P9-CFM-792

the TWELVE

LESLIE B. FLYNN

This book is designed for your personal reading pleasure and profit. It is also designed for group study. A leader's guide with helps and hints for teachers and visual aids (Victor Multiuse Transparency Masters) is available from your local bookstore or from the publisher.

VICTOR BOOKS

a division of SP Publications, Inc.
WHEATON, ILLINOIS 60187
*Offices also in* Fullerton, California • Whitby, Ontario, Canada • Amersham-on-the-Hill, Bucks, England

Unless otherwise noted, Scripture quotations are from the King James Version. Other quotations are from the *New American Standard Bible* (NASB), ©1960, 1962, 1963, 1968, 1971, 1972, 1973 by the Lockman Foundation, La Habra, California; *The Holy Bible: Revised Standard Version* (RSV), ©1952 by the Division of Christian Education of the National Council of the Churches of Christ in the United States; *The New Testament in Modern English* (PH), ©J. B. Phillips 1958, The Macmillan Company. Used by permission.

Recommended Dewey Decimal Classification: 232.95
Suggested Subject Headings: APOSTLES; BIBLE—BIOGRAPHY; DISCIPLES; SAINTS

Library of Congress Catalog Card Number: 81-86289
ISBN: 0-88207-310-9


Printed in the United States of America

VICTOR BOOKS
A division of SP Publications, Inc.
P.O. Box 1825 • Wheaton, Illinois 60187

# Contents

**To our good friends,**
**Carl and Violet Larsen**

# 1

# The Twelve

The teacher of an adult Sunday School class asked his class members to name the 12 Apostles. "That's easy," they exclaimed, then proceeded to call out, "Peter, James, John." Then with hesitation they added, "Andrew . . . , Thomas . . . , Judas. . . ." More silence, then, "Philip . . . Nathanael. . . ." No one could name the others. The average church member cannot name more than half of the Twelve. Some mistakenly include Mark and Luke.

Many churchgoers have wrong ideas about the Twelve. A group of tourists in Europe gazed at the stained glass windows of a lovely church. Each window displayed the portrait of a different apostle. Noting halos around their heads, their angelic expressions, and beautiful smiles the guide remarked, "What saints the apostles must have been!" But this is a misconception.

## Ordinary Men

Though the centuries have turned the apostles into unapproachable supermen, they were ordinary men. They were real people, faltering mortals who lived on Second Avenue in some Galilean town. They looked like some long-forgotten classmate whose picture appears in your high school yearbook, fourth from the end in the third row, whose name you can't recall. They would have had average schooling at their local synagogues.

They weren't old men, but youths, probably in their 20s, perhaps John in his late teens, and Peter near 30. We know Peter was married (Matt. 8:14). The Bible suggests the other apostles also had wives (1 Cor. 9:5). They came from the lower or middle classes, earning their livelihood by ordinary occupations. They were all Jews.

## Imperfect Men

The Gospels picture the apostles as men with imperfections and weaknesses. For example, they became afraid in a violent storm on the Sea of Galilee.

In Gethsemane they fell asleep when they had been especially asked to watch and pray.

Part of their indignation at Mary's anointing Jesus with costly perfume may have sprung from envy at her wealth (Matt. 26:8).

The apostles suffered lapses of memory like all of us. Once after crossing the Sea of Galilee, they discovered they had forgotten to bring bread (16:5).

Jesus had to rebuke the disciples for their unbelief which stood in the way of their casting out demons from a possessed child.

Two of their number wanted to incinerate a town (Luke 9:54).

They entertained false conceptions. They thought a man's blindness was caused by sin, either his or his parents'.

How slow they were to grasp their Master's teaching. "Fools and slow of heart" was an epithet that frequently fitted them.

They mistakenly blocked mothers from bringing their babies to Jesus for His blessing.

Arrogantly all boasted they would never deny Jesus, but would even die for Him. At His arrest they all forsook Him and fled.

Yet these are the men whose weaknesses and failures were transformed by the Master into strengths that made them collectively the foundation of the church (Eph. 2:20). The truth is—Jesus had to be content with these bumbling men. To accomplish His mission He had to ultimately rely on these simple, sincere, rustic, but enthusiastic, energetic followers. Slowly but surely through His patient training they grew in grace and wisdom till the day their Master ascended, leaving them to carry out His mission.

Their example should inspire hope in us. If the Lord can use a group of men, not exceptionally talented, nor unusually sainted, then all of us can become useful in His service. Though we cannot preach like Peter, nor write like Matthew, nor witness like Andrew, there's a place in the church for all people, despite their faults and frailties.

Many apparent failures turn out to be eminently successful. The teachers of Thomas Edison told his parents that their son was too stupid to learn anything.

A 21-year-old youth, working in a dry goods store, was judged by his employers unfit to meet the public. His name, F. W. Woolworth.

Walt Disney was fired by a newspaper because he "had no good ideas." When he took his drawings to a famous editor, he was told he had no real talent.

Robert Browning submitted a volume of poems to a famous London editor who, reviewing them, wrote across the front, "Froth, nonsense, trash."

The apostles in their early days seemed like a nondescript group headed for oblivion, but through association with Jesus ultimately turned the world upside down.

## Chosen Men

Jesus had numerous disciples, at least 70 whom He sent out on one occasion (Luke 10:1). From this larger group He issued a special call to 12. "And it came to pass in those days, that He went out into a mountain to pray, and continued all night in prayer to God. And when it was day, He called unto Him His disciples: and of them He chose twelve, whom also He named apostles" (6:12-13).

By what criteria He made His selection we are not told. But after some months of observation, He chose the Twelve.

*Meaning of apostle.* According to Kittle's *Dictionary of the New Testament, apostle* in classical Greek first denoted the dispatch of a fleet or army on a military expedition, then referred to the fleet itself, then finally to any group of men sent out for a particular purpose. It signified an authorized representative, officially duly accredited. By New Testament times an apostle was a person sent out with a message at the commission of a supreme power. In its verb form it means literally "to send off."

Mark wrote, "He ordained twelve, that they should be with Him, and that He might send them forth to preach, and to have power to heal sicknesses, and to cast out devils" (3:14-15). The 12 Apostles were fully accredited representatives with a specific commission, initiated by Jesus' will and accompanied by His authority (Matt. 10:1; Luke 6:13; Acts 1:2; 2:37, 42-43).

*Qualifications of apostles.* Certain qualifications made their office unique.

1. They accompanied Jesus from the beginning. When Peter called for a replacement for Judas' apostleship, he said the successor should be chosen "of these men which have companied with us all the time that the Lord Jesus went in and out among us, beginning from the baptism of John" (Acts 1:21-22).

2. They were among those who saw Jesus after His resurrection. Again in anticipating Judas' replacement, Peter said he must "be a witness with us of His resurrection" (v. 22).

3. They laid the doctrinal foundation of the church. Jesus promised to send His Spirit to guide the apostles into all truth. One major fulfillment of this promise was the New Testament revelation inspired by the Holy Spirit. Later-century believers admitted into the sacred canon only those writings which they knew emanated from the apostles or their immediate circle like Mark, Luke, and James.

4. They laid the structural foundation of the church. This involved the use of the keys (Matt. 16:18-19). Led by Peter, they opened the door of the Gospel, not only to Jews (Acts 2:38-41), but to half-Jewish Samaritans (8:14-17), and to Gentiles in Cornelius' household (10:44-48), and in Antioch (11:22-23). Apostolic approval was sought for each successive step of the Gospel as it proceeded outward beyond Jewish limits.

5. They had power to work miracles (Acts 2:43; 5:12; 8:18).

The purpose of this miraculous power was to authenticate their message (2 Cor. 12:12; Heb. 2:4).

In its official usage the term *apostle* is restricted to the Twelve, who uniquely possessed these qualifications (Acts 9:27; 1 Cor. 15:7). When the apostles died, the office of apostleship, in its narrow meaning, died with them. Though *apostle* is used in a broader sense, as in the cases of Barnabas, Silas, Timothy, and Paul, none of these possessed the criteria of the restricted Twelve.

Paul is an example of a person called an apostle, yet not among the Twelve. Many propose that Paul with his strong claim to apostleship, not Matthias, should have been named the replacement for Judas. Yet the validity of Matthias' appointment seems never to have been questioned by the apostles of the church. Matthias evidently acted in concert with the other eleven (Acts 2:14; 6:2; 9:27). Matthias will likely be one of the Twelve judging the 12 tribes of Israel. Matthias' name, not Paul's, will probably be inscribed on the foundation of the New Jerusalem (Rev. 21:14).

Though Paul emphatically claimed to be an apostle appointed by the Lord Jesus, and the recipient of special revelations, as well as a witness of the risen Christ, he did not qualify for apostleship in its restricted, official sense. Paul was never in the company of Jesus during His earthly ministry, much less from the baptism of John. Paul never claimed the right to be numbered among the Twelve, nor was he so appointed. Rather he recognized the Twelve as a group separate from himself (1 Cor. 15:5, 7).

## They Were Twelve

The Lord chose 12 apostles. Why 12? He could have made the apostolate smaller, or certainly utilized more.

Some Bible teachers point out that 12 is the number of the world (4), times the number of the Trinity (3), thus symbolizing the involvement of God in the human family. Also, 12 has been called the number of governmental perfection. God's chosen people were divided into 12 tribes. Also there will be 12 thrones for judgment on the tribes of Israel, 12 pearly gates in the New

Jerusalem, 12 foundations to the city, and 12 manner of fruits (Matt. 19:28; Rev. 21:12; 22:2).

Aware of the importance of their number as 12, the apostles were quick to fill the vacancy caused by the loss of traitor Judas (Acts 1:15-26).

Significantly, the apostles were often referred to as a corporate body, called the Twelve (Matt. 10:5; 26:14, 20, 47; Mark 4:10; 6:7; 9:35). They constituted a special body of believers, called and trained for a major, common mission. They acted together over and over, baptizing for Jesus, distributing the loaves and fishes to the 5,000, celebrating the Passover, and meeting the risen Christ in the Upper Room. Thomas' absence was noted from the first Easter meeting.

Again, in the early church they acted in community. All gathered in the Upper Room after the Ascension to await the Spirit's descent. It was at the apostles' feet that willing givers offered their gifts (Acts 4:37). All the apostles did signs and wonders (5:12-16). At Stephen's death the apostles remained in Jerusalem while most other saints scattered elsewhere (8:1). When groups beyond Jewry received the Gospel, the apostles wanted an accounting (8:14; 11:1, 22). Together the apostles questioned the validity of Paul's conversion (9:26-28). The apostles along with the elders formed the first church council (Acts 15:6; 16:4).

*Listings of apostles.* Four lists of apostles are given, one in each of the three synoptic Gospels (Matthew, Mark, and Luke), and one in Acts. For some reason John's Gospel does not have a list. These 12 names seem to form into three groups of four each, with each of the three groups always containing the same four names, though not in the same order.

However, each of the three groups always begins with the same name, perhaps indicating a recognized leader for that group. Peter stands first in group one (names 1-4). Philip stands first in group two (names 5-8), thus is always fifth, while James, son of Alphaeus, stands first in group three (names 9-12), thus is always ninth. Judas is always last except in Acts by which time he has committed suicide, and is therefore omitted.

Of the first group, three enjoyed a special relationship with

| Matthew 10:2-5 | Mark 3:16-19 | Luke 6:14-16 | Acts 1:13 |
|---|---|---|---|
| 1. Simon (Peter) | Simon (Peter) | Simon (Peter) | Peter |
| 2. Andrew | James | Andrew | John (RSV) |
| 3. James | John | James | James (RSV) |
| 4. John | Andrew | John | Andrew |
| 5. Philip | Philip | Philip | Philip |
| 6. Bartholomew (Nathanael) | Bartholomew (Nathanael) | Bartholomew (Nathanael) | Thomas |
| 7. Thomas | Matthew | Matthew | Bartholomew (Nathanael) |
| 8. Matthew | Thomas | Thomas | Matthew |
| 9. James the Less | James the Less | James the Less | James the Less |
| 10. Lebbaeus (Judas; Thaddaeus) | Thaddaeus (Judas; Lebbaeus) | Simon (Zealot) | Simon (Zealot) |
| 11. Simon (Zealot) | Simon (Zealot) | Judas (Lebbaeus; Thaddaeus) | Judas (Lebbaeus; Thaddaeus) |
| 12. Judas Iscariot | Judas Iscariot | Judas Iscariot | --- |

the Master. Only Peter, James, and John were privileged to see the raising of Jairus' daughter, the Transfiguration, and Jesus' agony in Gethsemane (Mark 5:37; 9:2; 14:33).

The apostles seem to be listed in the order in which they were converted and called. At least the first four—Peter, Andrew, James, and John—were the first to be called to follow Jesus. Then came Philip and Nathanael (John 1:40-45).

*In pairs*. Not only do the Twelve seem to divide into groups of four, but the quartets seem to break into pairs, making six sets of twos. Both the Seventy and the Twelve were sent out in couples (Luke 10:1; Mark 6:7). By traveling in pairs, each could encourage the other in times of loneliness, discouragement, and persecution, thus sympathizing with as well as encouraging one another.

How were the apostles paired off? Peter and John were often together preparing the Passover (Luke 22:7-8), running to the empty tomb together (John 20:2-4), going up to the temple to pray (Acts 3:1), speaking to the people together (4:1), imprisoned together (v. 3), bold together (v. 13), and reporting back to the church together (v. 23). This would put Andrew and James together.

Since Matthew links the disciples by pairs, he may well be spelling out the other usual groupings. But in different journeys and assignments the composition of the couples might have varied, thus accounting for the other Gospel writers' different order of names within the three groups of four. The chapters of this book follow the order of the apostles given in Matthew's listing.

Scholars suggest that Jesus' knowledge of personality, character, and temperament shows up in the way He paired the disciples; for example, putting outspoken Peter with meditative John. Or cautious, calculating Philip with guileless Nathanael, a man of simple faith. Or Thomas, a man of questions with Matthew, a disciple with strong conviction. Such well planned matching would strengthen each other's virtues and offset each other's deficiencies.

## They Were Transformed

Peter Marshall in a sermon, *Disciples in Clay,* pictured the apostles appearing before an examining board appointed to choose Jesus' close associates. Peter stood there smelling of fish, uncouth and uncultured, impulsive and impetuous. Andrew, James, and John also reeked of fish oil, and lacked refinement. Philip appeared indecisive. Thomas radiated cynicism. Matthew was considered a traitor to his country. Zealot Simon was a dangerous revolutionary. Judas was a thief. Without whitewash the New Testament paints them as they were, a group not "most likely to succeed." It's likely some of the disciples would not have chosen each other to be members of the group.

Over and over again they displayed bumbling ineptitude. Slow to understand Jesus' public discourses, they had to repeatedly ask Him to explain in private (Mark 4:10; 10:10). Their expectation of an imminent, earthly kingdom with emancipation from Rome was still deeply embedded up to the time of His Ascension.

The apostles couldn't grasp Jesus' predictions of the Resurrection. An early reference may have been somewhat veiled, "Destroy this temple, and in three days I will raise it up" (John 2:19). But later predictions with specific statements of a third-day resurrection were unequivocably clear (Mark 9:31-32; 10:32-34). Yet they didn't understand (Luke 9:45). When the Resurrection *did* take place, the apostles didn't believe it at first. But Jesus' enemies so believed His prophecies that they requested the sealing of His tomb by Roman authorities (Matt. 27:62-66).

*They were teachable.* To get across His message to mankind required pliable, childlike, unpretentious followers. He couldn't choose know-it-all scholars, millionaires, or socialites for they likely wouldn't be humble enough. Though slow to learn, they had to be willing to learn. If filled with their own knowledge, they would have no room for His wisdom. So, He chose men humble enough to be teachable.

A high school senior, desperately wanting admission to a certain university, wrote on her application, "I'm not a leader, but I think I'm a good follower." The admissions officer replied,

"Applications for our freshman class indicate that there are 599 leaders coming to the college next fall to fill 600 openings. We feel that the college is required to admit one follower. Please be advised that your application is accepted." How wise that not all the apostles were dynamic leaders.

*They were trained.* An article in *Psychology Today* (May, 1981) asked, "Does Personality Really Change after 20?" It pointed out that, contrary to William James who said that by age 30 character has set like plaster and will never soften again, the rallying cry of the 1970s has been people's virtually limitless capacity for change. The yippies of the 60s became establishment bankers and lawyers in the 70s. The article concluded that all of us reflect, over time, both stability and change. Though friends meeting us years later may remark, "It's the same old Bill," yet midst the essential coherence of personality is the potential for growth and change.

The Master brought many influences to bear on the Twelve in order to mold them into the men He wanted them to be. This curious assortment of followers could easily have each developed an inferiority complex. But after three years of His constant company they were transformed men, ready to carry out their assignments.

One aspect of Jesus' training was to give the apostles a vision of their potential. He let them know He understood their individual weaknesses, then held before them what they could become in the days ahead. At His first meeting with Simon, He dramatically called him what he was not—"rock." Simon knew the Lord had pinpointed an area of weakness in his life, his impulsiveness and instability. But Simon also received hope through his new name, for it indicated what he could and would become through divine power.

When Jesus called James and John "sons of thunder," He was letting them know He was aware of their fierce, fiery intolerance. He was also indirectly promising them improvement in that sphere of need. Several apostles had double names. Though we cannot be sure, perhaps other names like Simon's, were given by the Lord for the purpose of encouragement. Was Matthew, which means "gift of God," given Levi, the despised tax collector, to let him know he had a full and free pardon for all his shady past? Knowing the particular needs of each apostle, Jesus fashioned His instruction accordingly.

To help the "dull-witted" apostles learn, Jesus had to exhibit maximum patience. For instance, they took forever to learn the lesson of humility. When they argued over who would be greatest in the coming kingdom, He put a child in their midst, and exhorted them to be childlike (Mark 9:34-37). When the disciples failed to learn the lesson of childlikeness, rather still openly aspiring to the two top positions in the kingdom, the Master taught the ideal of servanthood, citing His own example of coming to minister, not to be ministered unto (10:35-45). But when they were still arguing over top rank right to the eve of the Cross, He gave them a graphic object lesson in humility by washing their feet in the Upper Room.

Not only did Jesus arouse expectation of character transformation, and not only did He exercise much patience with these slow learners, but He used many other methods of training. He taught by example as they watched Him deal with sinners. They heard Him pray so effectively that they came and asked, "Lord, teach us to pray" (Luke 11:1). They observed His love for the poor and needy. He sent them out on practical work assignments two by two, then required them to tell about all the wondrous things which God had done through them.

They lived in His presence for three continuous years of concentrated schooling. They heard His matchless words, saw His startling miracles, observed His unerring rectitude.

He was the Master Teacher, using questions to lead them on to discovery of truth. He illustrated remote truth by near-at-hand objects like sheep, lilies, vines, branches, candles, shepherds, sparrows, wheat, tares, nets, fish, leaven, bread, and seed. He saturated His teaching with stories.

Major topics of His teaching included the nature of the kingdom, prayer, true righteousness, His own Person and claims, the Cross and Resurrection, humility and related virtues, self-sacrifice, the dangers of Pharisaism, and the mission of the Holy Spirit to convince the world and to enlighten themselves.

To train them Jesus spent more time with them than with all other people combined. He ate, slept, and talked with them. Together they walked country roads, entered crowded cities, sailed the lovely Sea of Galilee, and worshiped in synagogues and temples. Through uninterrupted companionship He wanted to fashion them into a select band who after His departure would carry His message to Jerusalem, Judea, Samaria, and to the ends of the earth. He wished His church founded on deep convictions, not on superficial observations. He desired not just traveling companions, but flaming evangels to carry the Gospel of repentance and remission of sins worldwide.

How well did they learn? How wisely did He train them?

*They were changed.* People could not live in the presence of Jesus for three years and remain unchanged. Simon made major strides in his character transformation from clay to rock. John, who on one occasion wanted to incinerate a city, became the apostle of love. The rabble-rousing zeal of Simon the Zealot was channeled into enthusiasm for the Gospel. Some regard the transformation of the apostles almost the greatest of His miracles.

Through the Master's training, apostles on different sides of the psychological, temperamental, and political fences were melted into a Spirit-born oneness, even as Christ had prayed, "that they may be one" (John 17:22).

Two of Jesus' disciples were radically opposed idealogically. Matthew had sold himself into the service of Rome as a tax collector, thus earning the reputation of traitor to Jewry. Simon the Zealot had belonged to the revolutionary, anti-Roman freedom-fighters. Perhaps in their early days as the Twelve, Jesus had to step between them once or twice to prevent their animosities from flaring into fisticuffs.

On the first day of Congress in 1981, Speaker Tip O'Neill for the Democratic Majority responded to Republican Minority Leader Robert Michel, "as one of my closest social friends. Such friendship is one of the great things, I believe, that this nation has to offer, and you new members will ultimately learn . . . that there are many nations of the world where those who are of different parties do not speak to each other. You will find that they look at Americans and say, 'This is unbelievable—that members of the two parties of the Congress of the United States may differ philosophically and still seem to be close friends!' " Dr. Robert Dugan, editor of *Insight*, commented, "Evangelicals could learn from these politicians. How painful to see some Christians express disdain, and even hatred, for brothers or sisters in Christ who hold political office and disagree with them" (Feb., 1981).

A sculptor who had just carved a magnificent horse was asked the secret behind his work of art. "I just chipped away anything that didn't look like a horse," he replied. The Lord Jesus kept dealing with anything in the apostles that didn't resemble godliness.

The apostles became fitted for their spiritual, universal mission. In the final paragraph of his massive classic, *The Training of the Twelve*, A. B. Bruce says they were "enlightened in mind, endowed with a charity wide enough to embrace all mankind, having their conscience tremulously sensitive to all claims of duty, yet delivered from the fetters of custom, tradition, and the commandments of men, and possessing tempers purged from pride, self-will, impatience, angry passions, vindictiveness, and implacability."

When their exceptional training was anointed with the coming of the Holy Spirit at Pentecost, this nondescript, ragtag, dullish, fearful, unlearned gang of throne-climbers and deserters was transformed into a revitalized, united, godly band of flaming and courageous evangelists. The Book of Acts records how they took the Great Commission seriously and acquitted themselves magnificently. As a result of the tutelage of the greatest Fisher of men, they were able to cast the net of heavenly truth into the sea of the world, and to capture a great multitude of believing souls for the divine kingdom.

Tradition says the apostles decided on a strategy of world evangelism. They began by dividing the known world into zones of influence and responsibility among themselves. Then each traveled his separate way, thus together covering all points of the compass. The apostles were churchmen, organizing bodies of believers wherever they went.

Tradition has a field day with their travels and modes of martyrdom. Though the facts are cloudy, here is one suggested list of how the apostles met their deaths:

Peter, crucified at Rome, head downward.

James, beheaded at Jerusalem (Acts 12:2).

John, plunged into a boiling cauldron during persecution under Emperor Domitian, from which he was miraculously saved, later to be banished to the Isle of Patmos (where he wrote the Book of Revelation), from which he was returned to Ephesus where he died a natural death.

Andrew, crucified at Patras, Greece on an X-shaped cross that now bears his name.

Philip, hanged, crucified, or stoned in Asia Minor.

Bartholomew, flayed alive and beheaded in Armenia.

Matthew, slain with a sword in Ethiopia.

Thomas, his body run through with a lance in India.

James the Less, thrown from a tower in Jerusalem, stoned, and clubbed, from which he recovered, then later sawed into pieces.

Judas (Thaddaeus/Lebbaeus), shot to death with arrows in Mesopotamia.

Simon the Zealot, fatally attacked by a mob near the Persian Gulf.

Judas Iscariot, a suicide.

An old legend imagines Jesus arriving in heaven right after the Ascension, welcomed by all the angels. Then the Angel Gabriel asks Jesus, "You suffered much, dying for the sins of mankind. Does everyone down on earth know it?"

"Oh, no," replied the Saviour, "just a handful of folks in Jerusalem and Galilee know about it."

"Well, Master," continued Gabriel, "what is Your plan for everyone to know of Your great love?"

The Master replies, "I asked all My apostles to carry the message into all the world. I told them to tell others, who will in turn tell others until the last person in the farthest corner has heard the story."

Gabriel's face clouds, for he spots a flaw in the plan. "What if after awhile Peter forgets, and goes back to his fishing on Galilee, also James and John and Andrew. Suppose Matthew returns to his tax booth in Capernaum, and all the others lose their zeal and just don't tell others. What then?"

After a pause comes the calm voice of the Lord Jesus, "Gabriel, I have no other plan."

The apostles did their job well. But the Great Commission has not yet been fulfilled. The words of Jesus still weigh heavily on us today, "As the Father hath sent Me, even so send I you" (John 20:21).

# 2

# Simon Peter, the Rock

As Dr. Vernon Grounds finished his challenge to the Denver Conservative Baptist Seminary graduating class of '73, he presented each graduate with a tangible symbol as encouragement for his future ministry. Filing quietly to the front, the classmates wondered what it would be—a special Scripture verse, a little book, an inscribed medallion? It turned out to be a small square of white terry cloth towel. Says one graduate, who since has served as an overseas missionary, "We were commissioned to go into the world as servants. That small towel piece, frayed and grubby from years in my wallet, is a constant reminder of that moving moment and of our basic call to serve."

That miniature towel was an allusion to the night Jesus washed the disciples' feet after they had miserably failed to assume the servant posture. Simon Peter, who at first brashly refused to let Jesus wash his feet, received special rebuke from the Master, which he never forgot. That incident was just one of many that helped change him from shifting sand to solid stone.

## The Promise

Simon, originally from Bethsaida, moved to Capernaum where he and his brother, Andrew, were partners with James and John in a fishing business (John 1:44; Matt. 8:14; Luke 5:10). Like the other apostles, Simon never studied formally beyond synagogue school so was considered "unlearned" by the standards of the day (Acts 4:13). He was married. His wife and mother-in-law lived with him in a home co-owned by Andrew. This joint ownership suggests that their father, Jona, may have died (Mark 1:29-30; John 1:42).

Somehow we picture Simon as a man of rugged physique, with big, rough hands used to pulling heavy oars in strong seas, dragging boats to shore, and hauling drooping nets full of fish out of the sea. When he was in a boat with other fishermen, there was no doubt as to who was in command. He was a man of action and energy, a natural leader.

Though sturdy physically, he possessed a weak character. All four Gospels present him as impulsive, rash, hasty, impetuous, over-enthusiastic, sanguine, and swift to respond. Always asking questions, he became the spokesman for the Twelve (see chapter in author's book, *From Clay to Rock*, Christian Herald, 1981 on "Questions Peter Asked"). Simon swung his sword at Malchus' head, cutting off his ear. Simon ran right into the sepulchre, while the meditative John who had outfooted him to the tomb remained outside.

He talked when he should have been thinking. He slept when he should have been awake. He acted when he should have been still. Like the Sea of Galilee, he could erupt violently, then subside just as suddenly. Exasperating, though colorful, he blew hot and cold almost in the same breath. He dared to walk on water, then began to sink. He made a magnificent confession inspired by the Father, then rebuked Jesus with a remark that reeked of Satan. Though Simon told Jesus he would never let Him wash his feet, within moments he asked Jesus to wash him all over. He boasted that he would never deny Jesus, would even die for Him, but within hours declared with an oath that he had never met Jesus.

Jesus' first statement to Simon must have sounded strange, "Thou art Simon the son of Jona: thou shalt be called Cephas, which is by interpretation, a stone" (John 1:42). This was like calling a dwarf, "Goliath." Andrew thought, "My brother a rock? Doesn't Jesus know how unstable he is?" Perhaps Andrew had momentary doubt about the Messiahship of Jesus.

But Jesus never uttered any hasty, ill-timed statements. Before speaking to Simon, "Jesus beheld him" with a searching and all-knowing gaze (John 1:42). With deliberation He called Simon a rock. This new name indicated that Jesus clearly understood Simon's instability, and what He would make of Simon by His grace. Jesus saw Simon's potential.

To think of Simon only as an impulsive braggart is to do him an injustice. We should never forget this oscillating, vacillating fisherman became the solid, steady apostle who dominated the first half of the Book of Acts. Too many Christians liken themselves to Simon in the days of his failure. "I'm just so much like Peter," they say. "I deny my Lord too."

But for three years the Master chiseler chipped away at Simon. As the months passed, Simon became less and less Simon, and more and more Peter. The Resurrection and Pentecost added major finishing touches that produced a character in Acts so unlike the Simon that first met Jesus. But even then, sometimes the old Simon would assert himself. The Lord wanted to *Peterize* Simon, but so often the apostle *Simonized* Peter.

Instead of comparing ourselves to Simon, excusing our backsliding and unfaithfulness to God, we should compare ourselves to Peter, as he acted boldly in the early days of the church.

How did Simon's impetuous nature change from shifting sand to sturdy granite? Several incidents were involved in the transformation process.

## His Call

At first Simon alternated between fishing and part-time tours with Jesus. After Simon had fished all night without catching anything, Jesus came along and told him to thrust out a little from land and let down his *nets* (plural). Simon answered, "Master, we have toiled all the night and have taken nothing" (Luke 5:4-5). In other words, Peter was saying, "What do You, a carpenter, know about our trade? If we haven't caught anything during the night, we aren't likely to catch anything in the daylight." Then wavering between doubt and faith he added, "Nevertheless at Thy word I will let down the net" (v. 5). When Simon let down the *net* (singular), he caught so many fish that the net broke. Help was needed to get the catch to shore.

The miracle dazzled Simon. When Jesus called Simon to follow Him, his response was immediate. Along with Andrew, immediately joined by James and John, Simon renounced all for hardship and discipleship.

**Walking on Water** (Matt. 14:22-33)

Right after feeding the 5,000, Jesus insisted that the disciples precede Him by boat to the other side of the lake, knowing that they would row into a severe storm. The wind blew so hard that they only covered a maximum of three miles in a minimum of six hours, a speed of one-half mile per hour or less. In the darkest hour of the night, the predawn fourth watch, Jesus came walking on the water. Glimpsing this form moving majestically on the frothy, mountainous waves, the frightened disciples thought Him a ghost.

Identifying Himself, Jesus said, "Be of good cheer; it is I; be not afraid." Impulsively Simon cried out, "Lord, if it be Thou, bid me come unto Thee on the water" (Matt. 14:27-28).

Jesus didn't reply, "Foolish man. You ask the impossible," but rather, "Come." Jesus indulged Simon's impulsive whim, using it to develop firmer faith.

Simon started out magnificently. Climbing out of the boat, he began to walk on water toward Jesus. Then he panicked, his eyes wandered from Jesus to the waves, so that he started to sink. Immediately he cried out, "Lord, save me!" Jesus stretched forth His hand, grabbed Simon and said, "O thou of little faith, wherefore didst thou doubt?" (vv. 30-31) The hand that carved the mountains and flung the stars into space lifted Simon out of the water. Together, Simon and Jesus walked back to the boat.

Many people come down hard on Simon for his lack of faith. But Jesus didn't charge him with *no* faith, but rebuked him for *little* faith, an indirect acknowledgment of *some* faith. Remember—no other disciple showed any trust. Only Simon walked on water. If he only walked a yard before he sank, what a thrill he must have had. Whether Jesus had to hold Simon up on the return walk, or just hold his hand, how wonderful for him to experience buoyancy over tossing waves. His faith was growing.

## His Great Confession

One day Jesus asked His disciples a question, "Whom do men say that I the Son of man am?" They gave current theories: John the Baptist back from the dead, Elijah, Jeremiah, or one of the old prophets risen. But Jesus probed more personally, "But whom say ye that I am?" (Matt. 16:13-15)

Without hesitation, Simon confessed, "Thou art the Christ, the Son of the living God" (v. 16). Jesus affirmed that Simon received this revelation from His heavenly Father, then pronounced a blessing on him, "Thou art Peter, and upon this rock I will build My church; and the gates of hell shall not prevail against it" (v. 18). Whether the rock was Simon's confession, or Christ, or a combination of Christ and His apostles, Simon received the keys of the Gospel. This is why he was involved in the opening of the door for the Gospel to all three major groups: to the Jews at Pentecost (Acts 2:14-41), to the Samaritans (8:15-17), and to the Gentiles in Cornelius' household (10:25-48).

Soon after receiving this blessing, the same Simon was given a strong rebuke from Jesus. When the Lord spoke of His coming demise at Jerusalem, Simon took Jesus aside to rebuke Him, strongly denying such things would ever happen. Simon's remarks, in turn, brought vehement reaction from Jesus, who said, "Get thee behind Me, Satan" (Matt. 16:23). Then He added in effect, "Simon, don't you recognize you are striking right at the core of the Gospel? Without My death there'll be no forgiveness of sins. The path to the crown is by way of the Cross. Don't you see it's the devil who's prompting you to block the Cross?" (see vv. 24-27)

What a paradox! Just a few minutes earlier Simon had been congratulated as the recipient of a revelation from the Father. But next he was called a tool of the devil because he was trying to thwart Jesus' purpose. The rock was crumbling a bit.

## The Transfiguration

The disciples couldn't comprehend Deity dying. To remove the sting from His "death" announcement, Jesus promised that some would not die till they had seen the Son of man come with power. This promise was fulfilled a week later when Jesus gave Simon, James, and John a dress rehearsal of His coming glory.

Both the Lord's face and garments dazzled radiantly (Luke 9:29). Jesus' real self shone through. The outward splendor of His deity, which He had surrendered on coming to earth, burst forth. Though this sudden shining through of His glory was indeed a great phenomenon, its concealment for over 30 years was a greater marvel. Jesus walked around in the ragged disguise of humanity, hiding His splendid robes of royalty.

Simon was vitally strengthened by the Transfiguration. Jesus was indeed the mighty, glorious Son of God. Also, the appearance of Moses and Elijah plus their conversation corrected Simon's thinking (vv. 30-31). On the *person* of Jesus as the Son of God, Simon had earned an "A." But he flunked on understanding the *work* of Christ. Moses and Elijah, symbolic of Old Testament Law and Prophets, talked about the coming death of Jesus in Jerusalem, the very matter which Simon had contradicted. Now Simon learned that Jesus' death was of vital interest to the two Old Testament leaders. They agreed, though living 500 years apart, that in God's plan Jesus had come to die.

But Simon opened his mouth and put his foot in by suggesting the building of three tents for Jesus, Moses, and Elijah. While he was still giving his ill-timed advice, a bright cloud overshadowed them. The Father's voice boomed, "This is My beloved Son; hear Him" (vv. 33-35). The Son was not to be put on the same level with Moses and Elijah.

## The Question on Forgiveness

Simon was learning. One day he asked Jesus, "How often shall my brother sin against me, and I forgive him? Till seven times?" (Matt. 18:21) His suggestion of seven forgivenesses showed how far he had grown under Jesus' teachings. But he needed more chiseling. For he didn't anticipate the celestial arithmetic of forgiveness contained in Jesus' answer—"until seventy times seven" (v. 22).

To drive home the necessity of a forgiving spirit, Jesus told a story involving humorous exaggeration (vv. 23-35). A servant, about to be tossed into prison, successfully begged for mercy from his master to whom he owed a staggering debt of roughly $20 million. Then the forgiven servant refused a plea for mercy from a fellow servant who owed him a paltry $20, and threw him into jail. Whereupon the master threw the merciless servant into jail, canceling his earlier act of mercy and demanding his $20 million. Jesus ended the parable, "So likewise shall My heavenly Father do also unto you, if ye from your hearts forgive not every one his brother their trespasses" (v. 35).

A counselor asked a wife with marriage problems to bring in a list of her husband's good points, and a list of his bad points. The next week she brought in one sheet with a list of his fine qualities, but a one-inch thick notebook of grievances she had been recording for three years. Those who fill storehouses with grudges should recall Jesus' advice to Simon, "Forgive seventy times seven." Simon would stand in need of great forgiveness after his denial.

## The Foot-Washing (John 13:3-15)

A missionary once asked a group of national pastors in interior China what in Christ's life impressed them most. Various answers were given. None mentioned any miracle. Then one elderly man said, "His washing His disciples' feet." A general consensus showed that they were impressed that a reverend teacher would overstep the bounds of class and position to take a slave's place.

This episode also impressed Simon. That night in the Upper Room the disciples argued about who would have chief position in the coming kingdom. Common courtesy called for the washing of guests' feet. But since this was a loaned room, and the servants were busy elsewhere with Passover preparation, who would do the honors? In this atmosphere charged with feverish ambition, no aspiring disciple would stoop to kneel before his peers. Either with studied indifference, or unconscious ignorance each apostle looked the other way from towel and pitcher, regarding such a task beneath his dignity.

About this time Jesus rose from His place, discarded His outer garment, tied the towel around His waist, then performed the servant's chore. Silence settled over the room.

Simon thought such action demeaning to Jesus' dignity, so when Jesus reached him, Simon refused to let the Master wash his feet. Jesus replied, "If I wash thee not, thou hast no part with Me" (John 13:8). Desiring to share in the Master's work, Simon exclaimed, "Lord, not my feet only, but also my hands and my head" (v. 9). Swinging from one extreme to the other, Simon was exhibiting more sand than rock.

Jesus applied the lesson, "If I then, your Lord and Master, have washed your feet; ye also ought to wash one another's feet" (v. 14). The impression on Simon shows years later in his writings, "Yea, all of you be subject one to another, and be clothed with humility" (1 Peter 5:5).

When the sewerage system on a missionary complex backed up and created an awful stench, the senior missionary found two of his staff, the watchman and the chauffeur, arguing it was the other's responsibility to climb down into the slimy hole to clear out the pipe. Each deemed this repulsive task beneath his dignity. Without a word the senior missionary removed the manhole cover, and despite the nauseating odor, slid down into the sewer. The staff workers were so ashamed of their arrogant attitudes that they never again refused menial tasks.

## The Denial

The episode that revealed Simon's lack of rocklike reliability was his denial of Jesus. When Jesus warned that all the disciples would be offended because of Him, Simon replied, "Although all shall be offended, yet will not I." Then Jesus spoke specifically to Simon, "Verily I say unto thee, that this day even in this night, before the cock crow twice, thou shalt deny Me thrice." This only elicited more boasting from Simon who thought he was so strong, "If I should die with Thee, I will not deny Thee in any wise" (Mark 14:27-31). Though all said the same, Simon was the most dogmatic.

The Master knew Simon perfectly. But Simon didn't know his own weakness. After such warning Simon should have zealously begged for divine help, but spiritual negligence followed his misguided self-confidence. He slumbered both physically and spiritually. Asked to watch and pray in the garden, he could not stay awake. After the third bout of sleep the Master chided, "Simon, sleepest thou? Couldst thou not watch one hour?" (v. 37) In effect, "You who affirmed your love so loudly, could you not keep alert for just 60 minutes?"

At this point Simon should have cast himself on the Lord for strength. But moments later when a mob came to arrest Jesus, Simon lashed out with his sword, swinging at the nearest man, intending to make two out of him. But he missed and severed the right ear of Malchus, a servant of the high priest.

His momentary show of physical courage soon gave way to moral cowardice. First fleeing, then following afar off, he gained entrance to the courtyard, where he became one of the crowd warming himself at the fire. Perhaps he should have stood near Jesus, as John may have done. At least he should have stood up for Jesus in that crowd. But arrogant self-confidence, failure to watch and pray, fighting instead of submitting, and following afar off led to denial.

From a harmony of the four Gospels it seems that there were three periods of denial which became successively more intense. The first was a simple denial. The second was accompanied by an oath. The third was vehement, followed by cursing (Matt. 26:69-75).

When the cock crowed a second time and Jesus looked his way, Simon went out and wept bitterly. He was mostly clay, little rock.

## The New Simon-Peter

Simon slept little that night. The next day, he wept again and again, perhaps lurking in the outskirts of the crowd at the cross. Guilt burned in his soul through the Sabbath. He thought he was strong, but how much weakness there was: falsehood, evasion, ingratitude, cowardice, profanity, aggravated by the great privilege of three years with the Master, after solemn warnings, and in the hour of his Master's greatest need. This once proud disciple cringed like a whipped dog, almost beside himself with despair. How he needed a new lease on life to make him strong.

Early that first Easter came word from the Lord that cheered Simon's fallen spirit. An angel at the tomb had given this message, "He is risen . . . tell His disciples and Peter" (Mark 16:6-7). *And Peter.* Simon Peter could never forget that the angels singled him out by name! The Master still cared for him! Perhaps, after all, he could be forgiven!

Peter and John ran to the grave. Soon the truth dawned on Peter—Christ had *risen* from the dead. Sometime during that day, Christ confronted Peter privately. Doubtless Peter blurted out in full confession all the shame of his many denials. The Lord assured him of forgiveness, telling him to grieve no more.

Then in the next few weeks the Lord restored Peter publicly in the presence of the apostles. Around a morning fire on the shore of the Sea of Galilee, Jesus asked for a threefold affirmation of Peter's love. For each denial, Peter confessed his love. Peter's excessive self-confidence had been tripped up sufficiently to make him see his helplessness apart from Christ. The boastful man, humbled by his weakness, was qualified to strengthen his brethren. Three times he was commissioned, "Feed My lambs. Feed My sheep. Feed My sheep." Simon was now Peter (John 21:15-18).

Every backslider can take hope in Peter's restoration. In the Book of Acts, Peter was undisputed leader of the Twelve. He led the devotional exercises in the Upper Room, then directed the business meeting in which a successor to Judas was chosen. Later, on the Day of Pentecost, Spirit-filled Peter delivered a sermon that won 3,000 to Christ. He dominated the first twelve chapters of Acts, performing miracles, exposing Ananias and Sapphira as hypocrites, disciplining Simon the sorcerer, and evangelizing the household of Cornelius.

Under fire, Peter was imprisoned along with John for preaching Jesus as Christ. He made a magnificent defense under the guidance of the Spirit. Released, Peter and John were ordered not to speak nor teach in the name of Jesus. They replied they could not help but speak that name.

Jailed a second time, Peter was beaten and released. But he rejoiced that he was counted worthy to suffer shame for His name.

His third recorded imprisonment resulted in an all-night prayer meeting where believers begged the Lord to spare him from his execution scheduled for the next morning. The relaxed and sleeping Peter was awakened by an angel who knocked off his chains and opened the main iron gate. First going to the scene of the meeting to show the believers their prayer was answered, he then traveled elsewhere, not presuming on God's goodness. At this point Peter dropped off the pages of apostolic history, except for his testimony at the first church council at Jerusalem. There in opposition to Judaizing error, he joined Paul and Barnabas to affirm that salvation was by grace apart from the Law (Acts 15:7-11).

The rest of Peter's career is wrapped in mystery. Because a Cephas (Peter) party is mentioned in 1 Corinthians, it's likely he spent some time in Corinth (1:12). He concentrated some labor on the vast number of Jews scattered through Asia Minor, to whom he wrote his letters. He wrote his first letter from Babylon, which if taken literally means he visited there (1 Peter 5:13). Many believe Babylon is used as a code word for Rome to confuse Roman authorities on seemingly subversive prophecies about their empire, such as "Babylon the great is fallen" (Rev. 18:2). Tradition says Peter spent the last part of his life in Rome, dying a martyr, crucified upside down in fulfillment of Jesus' prediction (John 21:18).

The Simon of the Gospels seems so unlike the Peter of Acts. The changeable, cowardly Galilean became the courageous leader of the early church. It took months of pounding, hammering, and shaping on the anvils of God, months of molding by a patient Son of God. Jesus was always there, rebuking, commending, fashioning, warning, rescuing. A bulwark to his fellow apostles, Peter certainly lived up to his new name. Though in the Gospels he is frequently called by his *Simon* name, in Acts he is referred to as *Peter* almost exclusively (except for the purpose of identification, as in the Cornelius story).

Interestingly, when Simon's close friend John wrote his Gospel over half a century later, he used the two names together more frequently than separately (1:40; 6:8, 68; 13:6, 9, 24, 36; 18:10, 15, 25; 20:2, 6; 21:2, 3, 7, 11, 15). Since he knew Peter so well from earlier days, John could never escape using his old name *Simon*. But noting the marvelous metamorphosis through the years, he called him also by his deserved *Peter* title. Perhaps too a little bit of the old Simon cropped up now and again in the new Peter.

Old habits cling tightly, even to apostles. Before sending him to the Gentile Cornelius' household, the Lord reminded Peter that the distinction between Jew and Gentile had been done away with in Christ. To correct Peter's restricted outlook of the divine plan, the Lord gave him the vision of the great sheet containing unclean as well as clean animals.

Some years later, Peter wrongly withdrew fellowship from Gentile believers at Antioch when a strong Jewish group from Jerusalem arrived. But Paul challenged Peter to his face. Apparently Peter acknowledged his defection and reverted to the correct position on liberty. All the rest of Peter's life, as in yours and mine, the old and new natures would struggle, but the new progressively won out as clay became rock.

As Christ recognized in shaky Simon a solid stone, so He sees the potential character strengths we can have as He transforms us. Are you hot-tempered? If you come to Christ, He could call you *calm*. Are you a worrier? He might address you as *content*. Are you irritable, even ornery? He may call you *sweet*. Are you homosexual or adulterous? He might name you *pure*.

Character change became possible for Simon Peter when he met the Messiah. So for us, personality transformation requires that we open our hearts to the knock of Christ.

# 3

# Andrew, the Introducer

Moishe Rosen, founder of Jews for Jesus, introduced his wife, Ceil, to our congregation this way, "Ceil is not much of a soul-winner. The only folks she has ever won to Christ are her daughters and me."

The congregation laughed. Though Ceil Rosen may not have won many herself, by leading Moishe to Christ, she has been indirectly responsible for the hundreds that have found the Messiah through his ministry.

The Apostle Andrew worked quietly behind the scenes, winning people one by one. His brother Peter, always in the limelight, won 3,000 with one sermon. If Peter is called "the big fisherman," we would have to term Andrew "the little fisherman." But we should never forget that it was "the little fisherman" that landed "the big fisherman." Because Andrew labored privately, Peter preached publicly.

## Background

A native of Galilee, born in Bethsaida, Andrew was living in Capernaum at the time he met Jesus. He and his brother were not only partners in a fishing business on the Sea of Galilee, but they co-owned a house (John 1:44; Mark 1:29; Matt. 4:18).

But the brothers were so different. Peter roared like a firecracker, exploded into colors, then fizzled out. Andrew sizzled low with the constancy of a sparkler. Peter was impetuous, Andrew cautious. Peter led while Andrew followed. Andrew didn't fall emotionally at Jesus' feet after the miraculous catch of fish, nor did he jump daringly into the stormy sea to walk on water, nor rashly cut off a man's ear. Rather, he was solid, prudent, and conservative.

Though overshadowed by his brother, Andrew accepted his lowly spot, toiling on in relative obscurity. His name means *man*, though some translate it *manly* or *brave*. Andrew's name occurs 13 times in the Gospels and Acts. In three separate episodes, he brought people to Jesus. Not surprisingly, it was John, his close friend, who recorded all three instances.

### **His Conversion** (John 1:35-40)

As he fished day after day, perhaps Andrew meditated on the drastic differences between the religious practices of his time and the thunderings of Old Testament prophets. Then one day a prophet appeared on the scene preaching repentance. Tax collectors, soldiers, priests, zealots, and commoners all went to see this strange character dressed in camel's hair and eating locusts and wild honey.

Andrew was thrilled by this gaunt and intense personality who had emerged from the wilderness. Likely he was baptized by John. Hearing the Baptist declare himself merely a preparatory voice for a greater one, Andrew waited eagerly for the promised prophet. One day he saw the Baptist point to a man on the edge of the crowd and cry out, "Behold the Lamb of God, which taketh away the sin of the world" (John 1:29).

Irresistibly Andrew and an unnamed disciple, probably John, began to follow Jesus. Turning, Jesus asked, "What seek ye?" Perhaps at a loss for an answer, they replied, "Where do you live?" Jesus invited them to go with Him and see (vv. 38-39).

It would be wonderful if we had some record of their talk with Jesus. But whatever was said convinced Andrew that Jesus was the Christ. He decided to follow Jesus.

Andrew was the first to believe, along with John. The early

church called him Protoclete, or First-Called. To be first takes courage. It shows that Andrew wasn't afraid to follow his convictions. In quick succession the Gospel records the conversions of Peter, Philip, and Nathanael.

A never-to-be-broken allegiance to Jesus was established in that first encounter. Though Andrew went back to his fishing trade, he eagerly joined Jesus on sporadic trips. No persuasion was needed some months later when he heard the call of Jesus to full-time discipleship, "Follow Me, and I will make you fishers of men" (Matt. 4:19). Just as he had responded immediately to the invitation to salvation, so Andrew answered the call to consecration.

## His Personal Work

A pastor was asked, "If you had to win 100 people to Christ in the next 12 months, and were given the choice of doing it by either preaching or personal work, which method would you select?" Without hesitation he replied, "Personal work."

Andrew was a dedicated personal worker. Thrilled to find the Messiah, he couldn't keep the overwhelming discovery to himself. Though not much of a preacher like Peter who became the fisherman for the masses, Andrew became an effective fisherman on a one-to-one basis. Every time he came out of the biblical woodwork he was introducing someone to Jesus. Called *the introducer*, Andrew demonstrated that soul-winning need not be limited to preachers.

One historian said that in the early, fiery days of Methodism the intelligentsia would not hire a Methodist cook because she would seek to convert the housemaid, the kitchen maid, and all other "downstairs" personnel. In our day a Communist student on a college campus is given a list of approximately 20 other students he must try to win to Communism. The example of Andrew challenges Christians to exercise their soul-winning responsibility.

Andrew brought to Christ his brother, a boy, and barbarians. He began his witness at home, working outwardly from family to foreigners.

**He Brought His Brother** (John 1:41-42)
Immediately on finding the Messiah, Andrew began his life-pattern of soul-winning. First of all, he wanted his brother to know.

Simon, with his blustering ways and hot temper, seemed an unlikely prospective convert. But he respected Andrew's quiet, reliable, consistent ways. Andrew spoke with a joy in his soul and a certainty in his voice that could not be denied. He didn't half-heartedly whisper, "I saw a man who I think may possibly be the Christ." Instead he affirmed dogmatically and enthusiastically, "We have found the Christ!" The record adds, "And he brought him to Jesus" (v. 42).

True missionary work begins at home, admittedly often a difficult and discouraging field. Andrew began there with a brother who could not easily be told what to do. Often family members are skeptical about a new convert's faith in Christ. It may take time and fervent prayer before any positive results are seen.

When D. L. Moody was converted, his first thought was for his family, for whom he then began to pray. Previously he had sent home money and shoes, which as a shoe salesman he could buy at discount. But after his conversion, he wanted his family to share his new joy and peace.

Home for a few days to help with the potato planting, he tried to witness. They looked at him blankly, unable to comprehend what he was driving at. One of his sisters murmured she would be a Unitarian till she died. It took Moody some time to win part of his family.

Some people would rather give $500 to missions than approach an unbelieving family member with the Gospel. If our reticence stems from inconsistent behavior, we should clean up our act. Peter advised that when trying to win family members to Christ, our manner of life should be so convincing that observers would be won without a spoken word (1 Peter 3:1-2). If our consistent testimony is rejected, we can only wait, keep on praying, and trust the Holy Spirit to do His work in His time. Remember—Jesus' brothers did not believe till after His resurrection.

One Sunday morning when I preached about Andrew, I ended by saying, "My last illustration is a living one. We have in our congregation two brothers by the names of Andrew and Peter. I've asked them to come to the pulpit and tell their story."

Andrew spoke first, reminiscing how he and his brother had grown up as best friends. About 10 years ago, he had received Christ as his Saviour. Wanting the same blessing for his brother, he invited him to a new coffee-house ministry in our church and led him to Christ.

Then Peter spoke, telling how at that time he had noted a change in Andrew's life. He told how Andrew had invited him to the coffeehouse and led him to Christ. Many in the audience were deeply moved by this modern illustration involving brothers with the same apostolic names.

Walking by a restaurant a businessman noticed a poor boy eagerly looking in, his face pressed flat against the glass pane. "Are you hungry?" asked the man. The boy timidly replied, "Sure am, Mister." Taking the lad inside, the man ordered a lavish meal for him. But the boy kept looking toward the outside, showing no interest in the delicious food. The man tapped him on the shoulder, "Why don't you eat? You said you were hungry." The boy answered, "See that boy looking in through the window. That's my little brother. How can I eat with him standing there looking at me like that?" The man brought in the younger boy. What a feast they both had!

Likewise family members still outside need an invitation to the Gospel feast.

### He Brought a Boy (John 6:1-11)

The second instance of Andrew introducing someone to Jesus involves the only miracle recorded by all four Gospels.

A great crowd had followed Jesus around the head of the Sea of Galilee. They were tired, hungry, and far from home. No cafeterias, diners, nor McDonalds were near. The disciples' suggestion was to "send the multitude away" (Matt. 14:15). Jesus, testing the Twelve asked, "Where shall we buy bread to feed this crowd?" Philip figured it out—200 pennyworth, the equivalent of a man's wages for 300 days.

Just then Andrew spoke up. He had a lad with him who had a lunch of five loaves and two fish. Andrew had befriended the boy, perhaps telling him about his fishing experiences on the Sea of Galilee. If the boy would give his lunch to the Master, thought Andrew, Jesus would do the rest. Though the amount of food seemed so small, the Master miraculously multiplied it sufficiently to satisfy the appetites of 5,000 men plus women and children. Andrew provided the potential when he said, "There is a lad here."

We need Andrews today to bring boys and girls to Christ. An estimated 17 million children in the United States under the age of 12 have had no religious education. One million run away from home each year. Four out of ten children born in 1980 will live in a single-parent household for part of their childhood. An estimated million-plus boys and girls suffer abuse each year, with 50,000 dying from abuse during the past decade. Parents Anonymous, a self-help group for parents who have abused their children, now has 900 local chapters throughout the country.

Drinking alcoholic beverages has now reached our elementary schools. As many girls as boys use alcohol. Kids are not only drinking more, but they are consuming more when they get drunk. As early as 1979 the Department of Health, Education, and Welfare said that the number of teenage "problem drinkers" was 3.5 million and growing. Another study showed that 90 percent of today's teenagers have tried alcohol.

The only visible result of a week-long evangelistic crusade in a Scottish church was a little boy who stepped forward during the impassioned plea at the end of the final service. "Is this the best that can result from these meetings?" thought the pastor. Little did he realize that thousands would be won to Christ, and a whole continent opened up for the Gospel through that little fellow. His name was David Livingstone.

Gratitude and support are due the great many Christian youth movements in our country which try to bring young people on every age level to Christ. Significantly, Andrew has been called "the patron saint of Sabbath schools."

A painting, *The Martyrdom of St. Andrew* done by an artist

named Murillo, hangs in a European art gallery. At one side stands the figure of a boy with tears streaming down his cheeks, his face turned away as though unable to endure the terrible sight. Anachronistically, the artist had placed at the martyrdom the lad who had given his lunch. This boy felt he owed his soul to the influence of that friend who had brought him to Jesus, so was there in those awful moments to pay tribute.

### **He Brought Barbarians** (John 12:20-33)

Toward the end of His ministry, just a few days before the crucifixion, among those who came up to the feast at Jerusalem were "certain Greeks." (Though the world of that day was divided into Greeks and barbarians, the Jews considered everyone outside their nation to be aliens.) These strangers first approached Philip with the request, "Sir, we would see Jesus." Perhaps they came to Philip first because he had a Greek name and Greek connections.

Philip didn't know what to do. Christ's mission had been to win the lost sheep of Israel. Philip took the aliens to Andrew. Had he gone to Peter, James, or John they might have reacted, "Tell those Greeks to get lost! Jesus' message is for Jews only!"

But Andrew seemed not to be bigoted in any way. He had learned that his Master was no respecter of persons. Did he remember Jesus saying, "God so loved the world"? Somehow he saw the universality of the Gospel with its welcome for all mankind. It didn't matter to him that these people were outsiders. With Philip he introduced the Greeks to Jesus.

We're not told how the Greeks responded. But we do know that through Andrew's intervention they heard the Master speak of His coming death on the cross, of His drawing *all* men to Himself, and of His call to discipleship. Tradition suggests that Dr. Luke was one of those Greeks.

In a sense Andrew was the first foreign missionary. In fact, because he also began his witness at home base, he has been given the title of "Home and Foreign Missionary."

But our soul-winning efforts must not stop at home. The Great Commission demands our participation in the worldwide mission of the church. A lot of Andrews will be necessary before the whole world knows.

## Andrew's Willingness to Take a Secondary Spot

A competitor at a flower show was given second prize. But right in front of the spectators he ripped the award ribbon into shreds in a fit of jealous anger. He could not take second place. But Andrew could.

Andrew was known as the brother of Peter. In two listings of the Twelve he appears fourth (Mark 3:18; Acts 1:13). In the other two he is mentioned second, immediately after Peter and termed Peter's brother (Matt. 10:2; Luke 6:14). He is also called Peter's brother when he brought the boy with his lunch to Jesus (John 6:8). The implication was that people might not have known who Andrew was, so he was identified as Peter's brother, for everybody knew Peter. How did Andrew react to Peter's preeminence, especially since he had introduced Peter to Jesus?

Moreover, Andrew never did quite make that inner circle who were privileged to witness the raising of Jairus' daughter, the Transfiguration and the garden agony. Andrew was excluded.

His exclusion is reminiscent of one of King David's mighty men, Benaiah. After recounting his brave exploits, the sacred record adds, "He was more honorable among the thirty, but he attained not to the first three" (1 Chron. 11:24-25). Likewise Andrew, more honorable than the other eight, did not attain to the top three. How did he feel, knowing that he was a believer before those other eight?

Andrew must have been a humble fellow. At first, like the others, he may have aspired to top position in the kingdom. But at some point, realizing he was not going to play a main role, he quietly took his place as a stagehand. It was enough that the Master considered him worthy of a place among the Twelve. Perhaps he would have failed as a member of the inner three. To be relegated to a secondary spot did not bother him.

Perhaps he learned humility from John the Baptist who willingly took second spot to Jesus as a voice, not the Word, as forerunner, not the Messiah. How wrong to have ill-will toward a superior, a better athlete, a brighter student, a prettier lady, or a better emcee. Andrew thought more of service than of reputation. As long as the job got done, it didn't matter who got the credit.

Andrew went quietly about his job, winning people one-by-one. The "Andrews" of our churches seldom preach from influential pulpits. They teach small Sunday School classes, lead small Bible study groups, or direct small youth fellowships. The church needs its few "Peters" and "Johns." But it cannot get along without its multitude of "Andrews," ministering faithfully behind the scenes.

Three countries claim Andrew as their patron saint: Russia, Scotland, and Greece. Tradition says that he died at Patrae, Greece, when the local governor, enraged because his wife and brother had become Christians, condemned him to crucifixion. Tradition also says that Andrew, feeling unworthy to die on the same-shaped cross as his Master, suffered martyrdom on an X-shaped cross, later called St. Andrew's cross. He supposedly lingered for three days, trying to lead people to Jesus during his conscious hours.

We never know how many souls may be won to the Lord through those we win. Dr. Peter Joshua, pastor and evangelist, was won to Christ by the faithful witness of one girl. An unemployed actor, he slept in alleys at night and accepted handouts by day. One evening in London's Hyde Park, he saw a Salvation Army girl stand up as if to read poetry. Wanting to give her support, he found himself her only audience. Instead of reading poetry, she began to sing. It was a hymn that showed the worthlessness of the world compared to the glories of Christ. Looking Joshua straight in the face, she quoted several Bible verses, then turned and went her way. Right then, Joshua received Christ.

Years later when Dr. Joshua was the featured speaker at the sunrise service in Chicago's Soldiers Field, he wished that little Salvation Army girl could have seen him then. If only she could have realized that her faithfulness in speaking to one person was reaching out to 70,000 people in that great Resurrection celebration.

Andrew's name is associated with a systematic strategy to bring the unconverted to evangelistic campaigns, known as *Operation Andrew*. Christians are encouraged to list from 3 to 10 names of non-Christian friends, pray for each one regularly, then bring at least one each night to the campaign. Research indicates that most converts are brought to church and crusade services through individual invitation and concern.

Hank Beukema, a member of the Billy Graham organization for 10 years, was holding training sessions prior to a crusade in North Carolina. After the presentation of the *Operation Andrew* plan, a lady approached him, "I'm 82 years old. I haven't won anyone to Christ for many years. I've been trying to think of people to invite to the crusade, but I just don't seem to have any non-Christian friends."

A few nights into the crusade, he was standing at the front near those being counseled at the end of the service when he felt a tug on his coat. It was the same lady. "I've been going to the supermarket twice a day on purpose. I used to go only once a week. Every time I've gone this week I made sure I got the same checkout girl. I've become friends with her." Pointing to a girl at the front she added excitedly, "There she is. She's being counseled for salvation."

A few nights later, again at the front after the invitation, Beukema felt a tug on his coat. Again it was this lady. "How do I look?" she asked. Before he could answer that dangerous question, she continued, "I've been to the beauty parlor twice this week. I haven't been in years. I made sure I got the same operator. We became friends. She's over there being counseled."

If, like Andrew, we're going to win people to Christ, we must open our hearts, reach out warmly, and cultivate genuine friendships with those around us.

# James, the Hotheaded

A man, known for his terrible temper, couldn't get his car started one cold New England morning. Taking a wrench and lifting up the hood, he tried to adjust a part that had caused trouble for several days. But no matter what he did, the engine refused to start. Finally, he stepped back and threw the wrench full force right into the engine. Of course, that didn't start the car either. Instead, his temper tantrum resulted in serious damage that required major repairs.

Not long after that incident, the man became a Christian. The change, though not overnight, was unbelievable. He rarely lost his temper, for his Spirit-empowered self-control usually reflected the gentle nature of Christ.

This same kind of change came over the lives of two of the Twelve, James and John. They were brothers with such explosive tempers that Jesus nicknamed them "Sons of Boanerges," meaning "Sons of Thunder" (Mark 3:17). They were men of stormy disposition, tempestuous zeal, and fiery spirit. With low boiling points, their ready anger could erupt like a volcano. They have been described as hotheads who would shoot off their mouths before taking careful aim. But through association with the Master, John (whose story is told in the next chapter) was transformed into the apostle of love, and James became the first apostle to be martyred, suffering gladly for righteousness' sake.

## A Member of the Inner Three

Because it says Andrew "first" found his own brother, Simon, and brought him to Jesus, some infer that the other disciple, unnamed but probably John, also led his brother, James, to Jesus (John 1:41-42). Whether true or not, these two sets of brothers, all partners in a fishing business in Capernaum, accepted Jesus as their Messiah.

At first, these four alternated between their fishing vocation and part-time travel with Jesus. During that time, they witnessed the miracle of water changed into wine and the salvation of the Samaritan woman. Then came the call to full-time service. For James and John, it was while they were busy mending torn nets.

With them in the boat was their father Zebedee, apparently a prosperous man, for he owned boats and employed workers (Mark 1:19-20). Some think the family had business connections in Jerusalem, explaining why John seemed to know officials in the holy city (John 18:15). Doubtless Zebedee looked forward to the day when his two sons would take over the business. Born fishermen, they had been reared on the sound and smell of wind and waves, boats and sails, nets and fish.

But Jesus wanted them to catch men, quite different from catching fish. Fish when caught die, whereas men when captured for Christ become alive in Him. Jesus called, in effect, "Follow Me, and henceforth you will take men alive" (Matt. 4:24; Luke 5:10). In obedience the brothers left everything: father, boats, fellow-employees, fish, and business.

As Andrew took a back seat for Peter, so James sank into the shadow of his brother, John. James is never mentioned apart from John in the Gospels. John never mentions James at all. In his first mention in the Gospels, James is called the son of Zebedee; in the last reference he is called the brother of John (Matt. 10:2; Acts 12:2). James knew what it was to be introduced as the brother of some well-known person.

But surprisingly, James is named ahead of John in all four listings of the Twelve (Matt. 10:2; Mark 3:17; Luke 6:14; Acts 1:13). However, most versions other than the King James put

John before James in the Acts' listing. The reason for James' seeming priority is his seniority. Older than John, he was often termed by Bible scholars, "James the Great," or "James Major," or "James Senior."

Nevertheless James must have had special ability since the Master selected him as one of His inner three. We can understand why Peter was there—he was a born leader. And John was "the disciple whom Jesus loved." But why James? Undoubtedly he was capable and promising. Jesus must have considered him an honored and respected man with great potential.

The inner three were permitted to see and hear things the others didn't. With Peter and John, James stood in the death chamber of Jairus' daughter and watched wide-eyed as that cold, pale form sat up and then walked. Along with the other two, James saw Jesus transfigured, as a dazzling radiance flashed about His form and the Father's voice confirmed His Sonship. At close range James and the other two observed the Lord's agony, as He sweat drops of blood in anticipation of His bitter sufferings (Mark 5:37; 9:2; 14:33).

Because these three men were destined to be leaders of the early church, Jesus let them witness His power in raising the dead, His transfigured majesty, and His Gethsemane agony. Certainly these events helped prepare James for his role as the second recorded martyr (Acts 7:59-60; 12:2).

In examining the three following episodes, we see varying facets of James' strong-spirited nature: his vengeful zeal, his inordinate ambition, and his faithfulness unto death.

## His Vengeful Zeal (Luke 9:51-56)

Not long after the Transfiguration, and toward the close of His Galilean ministry, the Lord was leading his disciples through Samaria toward Jerusalem. He sent two advance men, James and John, to find the group lodging for the night. Picture the others, weary from trudging the dusty roads, the sun relentlessly beating down on them; eager for a cooling footwash, warm meal, and comfortable rest.

Suddenly the disciples saw James and John coming toward

them, agitated. The brothers reported that the villagers would not give welcome to any Jewish travelers, an illustration of the well-known animosity between Jews and Samaritans. This meant turning again to the open road to find some more hospitable place. James and John were fuming. Hungry and worn, they felt such unkind treatment should be avenged. Their hair-trigger tempers blew up. "Lord, wilt Thou that we command fire to come down from heaven, and consume them, even as Elijah did?" (v. 54) They wanted to wreak the fire and brimstone of Sodom on the Samaritans. No wonder Jesus called these brothers, "sons of thunder." Perhaps He should have called them "sons of lightning."

James and John used the precedent of Elijah. When 50 of King Ahaziah's men tried to arrest him, Elijah said, "Let fire come down from heaven and consume these men." And it did. A second contingent of 50 men suffered the same fate. When a third detachment came apprehensively, begging for their lives, Elijah finally agreed to go with them to the royal palace, convinced that the king would not dare hurt him (2 Kings 1:9ff).

When Jesus sent out the disciples two by two on their itinerant ministry, He told them, in effect, that if any place failed to give them food or lodging or hearing, that village would receive a worse fate than Sodom and Gomorrah (Matt. 10:14-15). James and John reasoned that if Sodom and Gomorrah had suffered destruction by fire from heaven, wouldn't Jesus approve their request for fire on the Samaritans?

The people of Samaria were a breed of half-Jews descended from Assyrians. Their presence was an embarrassment because they followed their own version of the Old Testament and worshiped at a rural temple at Gerizim. James and John thought they had a good right to get angry.

James' impure zeal was mixed with the fumes of pride and anger. His spirit of vengeful spite would have consigned his enemies to the place of fire. If James was to be a carrier of Jesus' Gospel, he needed a different spirit. So Jesus corrected him, "Ye know not what manner of spirit ye are of. For the Son of man is not come to destroy men's lives, but to save them" (Luke 9:56).

Somehow the Twelve had not yet learned that trading insult for insult would do no good. They forgot Jesus' words, "Love your enemies, bless them that curse you, do good to them that hate you, and pray for them which despitefully use you, and persecute you" (Matt. 5:44). They had been told to forgive seventy times seven. But James did not want to forgive even once.

How far James was from the spirit of Jesus' teaching and ministry. So often the Twelve had seen Jesus as the Friend of sinners, reaching out to the lost to offer pardon and hope. They had seen Him talking with a Samaritan woman by a well. She had had five husbands, and was then living with a man to whom she wasn't married. Yet Jesus revealed Himself to her as the water of life, after which she witnessed to others of her new-found Messiah. Somehow James had forgotten this magnificent example of Jesus' love for the half-breed Samaritans.

Jesus reinforced His teaching with His example. He didn't insist on being received by the villagers, but simply moved on to more receptive soil. We shouldn't be too hard on James, though. It's hard for almost everyone to accept insults graciously.

Just as Peter turned gradually from clay to rock, so hotheaded James grew out of this thunderous vindictiveness to caring concern for the Samaritans. Before His Ascension Jesus told the apostles they would be His witnesses, among other places, in Samaria (Acts 1:8). Early Acts tells of Peter and John preaching the Gospel "in many villages of the Samaritans" (8:25). Likely, James made missionary trips into the same region, perhaps into the very village which earlier had rejected him. Instead of calling down fire to burn their bodies, he called down the flame of the Spirit to indwell their hearts.

A *New York Times* article, "Religion Becomes a Part of Baseball Scene" (May 10, 1981), traced the growth of a spiritual movement on the San Francisco Giants team since 1978. While pointing out the tension in mixing evangelical beliefs with aggressive sports-playing, the story mentioned the change the "born-again" experience brought to many players.

Rob Andrews, an infielder in the minor leagues in the mid 1970s, was known for his bad temper. He once asked his manager to install a punching bag behind the dugout so he could punch away his frustrations. He joined the Giants in 1977.

His locker was next to Gary Lavelle's, a relief pitcher who led the spiritual movement in the Giants' clubhouse. Said Andrews, "I saw Lavelle go through hard times that would have killed me. But he always was calm. He never preached to me. But one day I asked him, 'Gary what is it?' He said it was Christ."

The manager of the Giants commented, "I saw Rob Andrews' life turn around. It was great." When Andrews, with a milder disposition, left baseball he became a youth pastor in California.

James' life was turned around so that he became a conqueror over his unruly spirit.

**His Excessive Ambition** (Matt. 20:20-28; Mark 10:35-45)
Though Jesus repeatedly told His disciples of His coming sufferings and death at Jerusalem, they didn't understand Him (Luke 18:31-34). Even on the final journey to the holy city, shortly before the crucifixion, the Twelve were thinking of the thrones promised them (Matt. 19:28). Approaching Jerusalem they thought the kingdom of God was surely about to appear, totally oblivious to the fact that Jesus' course would lead to collision with the authorities and to death.

But who would have the top throne? The hotheaded brothers had been doing some thinking. So to try to establish a pecking priority in the coming kingdom, they requested the two top spots. Perhaps Jesus' words to Peter about the keys of the kingdom (16:19) had shocked them into envy. With their wealth hadn't they given up more than any of the other disciples? With influential friends in Jerusalem, they felt themselves a cut above the others. So why shouldn't they get more honor?

The spirit of James often creeps into ecclesiastical circles today. Church officers have sometimes thwarted attempts to place on a board or committee a person whose achievements and talents might endanger their own supremacy. James' spirit surfaced later in the first century in Diotrophes, who was described as one "who loveth to have the pre-eminence" (3 John 9). It is a vain, self-seeking attitude which makes one want to become a church boss, lording it over their brethren. Greek professor A. T. Robertson once wrote an article on Diotrophes for a church magazine, portraying him as a church officer who wants to control a church according to his own whims. Subsequently 20 deacons from various parts of the country wrote the editor to cancel their subscriptions because of "this personal attack" made on them!

James and John enlisted their mother in the conspiracy. Like many over-ambitious-for-their-children mothers, she was a willing accomplice. Or perhaps she engineered the plot, approaching Jesus separately from her sons. She may have joined the Twelve at this time on her way to the feast at Jerusalem. Or, if her husband Zebedee had died by now, she may have been one of the group of women who often traveled with the Twelve, financially supporting Jesus' ministry (Luke 8:1-3).

Even though He had previously repeatedly emphasized the need for humility, Jesus' reply to this selfish, presumptuous request was quite mild. Patiently He put a question to them, "Ye know not what ye ask. Are ye able to drink of the cup that I shall drink of, and to be baptized with the baptism that I am baptized with?" (Matt. 20:22) In effect He told them that at this time He was not offering thrones but tribulation.

Scarcely realizing what would be involved in drinking the cup of their Master's sufferings, they glibly replied, "We can." James wouldn't have wanted to be on Jesus' left or right side when He was beaten with many stripes, or when He hung on the cross for six hours. But knowing that James would one day suffer for His sake, Christ said, "Ye shall drink indeed of My cup, and be baptized with the baptism that I am baptized with: but to sit on My right hand, and on My left, is not mine to give, but it shall be given to them for whom it is prepared of My Father" (v. 23). The assignment of honored seats was not at His disposal but belonged to the Father, who reserved them for those who earned them. But there would be no crown without the cross.

The request of James and John was not made too privately,

for the other 10 heard it, and became indignant against the 2. Pushy people are not popular, especially when pushing for what others want. The 10 were just as ambitious as James and John. See the halos fall as the Twelve engage in the unholy spectacle of arguing over the top positions.

Here was a major crisis. So, calmly the Master gathered the Twelve around Him to rerun a lesson he had given them umpteen times. Summed up—the leaders of the Gentile world govern people dictatorially and tyranically with no one to restrain them. But this is not the kingdom's way. Unbridled ambition is dangerous. Learn that the way up is the way down. Abasement brings exaltation, especially the humility of ministering to needs around us. To be chief, be servant. Then Jesus cited His incarnation as an example. The whole purpose of His coming into the world was not to be waited on, but to serve even to the point of death to save people from their sins (see vv. 25-28).

The disciples did not learn the lesson yet, for a short while later, right in the Upper Room the night before the cross, they would argue again who would be greatest. Finally, after the Resurrection and Pentecost the disciples were transformed from fiery, ambitious persons into men who made Christ their chief fire and ambition.

The church of the 20th century has people who seem to be hotheaded and have a tendency toward ambition. We need leaders today who will not abuse their position, but be accountable to their boards, acknowledge their weaknesses, set limits for their powers, and prefer one another in honor. Principal Cairns, headmaster of an English school, was assigned a seat at the front of a great gathering. As he walked in a line with other dignitaries onto the platform, his appearance was met by a burst of applause, for he was very popular. But Cairns stepped back to let the man behind him pass, then began to applaud his colleague. In his modesty he assumed the applause was for another, though it was really for him.

Like an unbroken colt, full of spirit and drive, James needed a higher power to control his life. His early martyrdom reveals how Christ channeled his energy.

## His Early Martyrdom (Acts 12:1-2)

A Roman coin pictures an ox facing both an altar and a plow with the words, "Ready for either." Such was the dedication of the Twelve, ready for sudden sacrifice or the slow routine of the plow. Though John was to labor in the Master's vineyard till his 90s, James suffered martyrdom about a decade after Pentecost. It's not how long, but how much we live.

Of the original Twelve we know how only two died, Judas tragically a suicide, and James by the sword, the second recorded martyr of the Christian era.

After the Resurrection James was one of the seven who went fishing, was among the apostles in the Upper Room, was present at Pentecost, and with the Twelve whenever mentioned as a group (John 21:1-2; Acts 1:13; 11:1). The only other reference to James is the mention of his death. "Now about that time Herod the king stretched forth his hands to vex certain of the church. And he killed James the brother of John with the sword" (Acts 12:1-2).

Why James? Herod Agrippa, grandson of the infamous Herod the Great, wishing to increase his popularity with the Jews and thus stabilize his political fortunes, instituted persecution against the church. Whom should he seize first? He chose James. The explanation seems to be that James with his zeal, zest, and ambition was a fiery, effective, and prominent leader. His zeal marked him for early arrest. Herod wished to silence his vibrant voice.

James' godly aggressiveness may have made him number one target even over Peter. Or perhaps Herod was testing his power. When the action against James was successful, Herod then imprisoned Peter, undisputed leader of the church (v. 3). Perhaps James was the most hated man by the Jews in Jerusalem. This outstanding apostle who preached with passion was the first to be arrested in this particular persecution. His flame would not die out, not even when apparently extinguished by martyrdom.

An old legend says that as James was arrested, his chief accuser was so deeply moved by James' courage and restraint that he begged for baptism and was admitted into the fellowship of the church, also dying at the same time as James. On the way to execution he implored James to forgive him. Without hesitation James embraced him, uttering, "Peace be unto you." The James of this legend is a far cry from the apostle who wanted to call down lightning on the insulters in that Samaritan village.

Why James was martyred, and Peter released from prison and spared Herod's cruelty, remains a secret of divine wisdom. Significantly, after James died, no vote was taken to fill up his vacancy, as had been done after Judas' suicide. When the original Twelve, with Matthias in Judas' place, were gone, no more apostles were appointed in their places. The office of official apostle died out with them.

Tradition says James made a voyage covering the entire Mediterranean, landing in Spain for a lengthy residence, where he founded many churches. This accounts for his selection as patron saint of Spain. His symbol is three scallop shells, representing his pilgrimage by sea.

James was a forerunner of untold thousands who through the centuries would die for their faith. A recent martyr given wide prominence in American newspapers was Charles Bitterman III, a missionary with the Summer Institute of Linguistics in Colombia, South America, overseas counterpart of Wycliffe Bible Translators. The linguist, who had just arrived in Bogota for gall bladder surgery, was seized by six terrorists on January 19, 1981. In an open letter to several Bogota newspapers, the terrorists stated their intention to kill Bitterman unless SIL completely withdrew from the country by February 19. But SIL had already agreed on a policy of never paying ransom or submitting to terrorist demands, reasoning that to capitulate in one instance would invite a rash of similar episodes everywhere. When the deadline passed without incident, hopes were raised. But early on March 7, six weeks after his kidnapping, Bitterman was found shot to death. His body was found on the floor of an abandoned bus on the outskirts of Bogota, wrapped in the red, white, and blue terrorist flag. He was buried by family and friends the same afternoon at a missionary base camp 100 miles southeast of Bogota.

The same page in *Christianity Today* which gave a column-and-a-half account of the Bitterman martyrdom also carried a half column report of a missionary couple found bound and stabbed to death in their Kabul, Afghanistan home. Eric and Eeva Barendsen had served more than eight years at the eye hospital with the International Assistance Mission. Hostility to foreigners had increased since the Soviet occupation. Their murders occurred during the anniversary week of that event. Despite the risk, the Barendsens had chosen to stay in Afghanistan. They had explained their decision by saying, "We are the only ones to love this people."

Undoubtedly, thousands of unknown, unhonored saints are dying for Christ every year around our world. Says the writer Reginal Heber in his hymn, "The Son of God Goes Forth to War:"

The martyr first, whose eagle eye
Could pierce beyond the grave,
Who saw his Master in the sky,
And called on Him to save:
Like Him, with pardon on his tongue
In midst of mortal pain,
He prayed for them that did the wrong:
Who follows in his train?

A glorious band, the chosen few
On whom the Spirit came,
Twelve valiant saints, their hope they
knew,
And mocked the cross and flame:
They met the tyrant's brandished steel,
The lion's gory mane;
They bowed their necks the death to feel:
Who follows in their train?

A noble army, men and boys,
The matron and the maid,
Around the Saviour's throne rejoice,
In robes of light arrayed:
They climbed the steep ascent of heaven
Through peril, toil, and pain;
O God, to us may grace be given
To follow in their train.

# 5

# John, the Beloved Son of Thunder

A *Wall Street Journal* headline in 1971 called Charles Colson the President's "hatchet man." He was considered a tough and macho troubleshooter, ruthless in getting things done. His axe-wielding skills included smear campaigns in the press against those who stood in the government's path. The article contained an unnamed source's observation that "Colson would walk over his own grandmother if he had to."

To see Colson in action today makes people wonder if he is the same man. As a result of serving a jail sentence, he has developed an enormous sympathy for prisoners. He founded Prison Fellowship which has reached into over 100 American prisons. In a recent year, 70 "In-Prison" seminars, each lasting a week, were held in 40 state and 30 federal institutions. Also in the same year 250 inmates graduated from Washington Seminar programs, which involved furloughed inmates spending two weeks of intensive Bible study and discipleship training in the nation's capital.

This transformation from tough to tender describes not only Charles Colson, but the Apostle John as well. Strangely, John has been portrayed in art as a mild-mannered youth, beardless and gentle. For example, Leonardo da Vinci's "Last Supper" pictures him full-faced, with an almost girlish smile, his white hands softly folded. Though he was likely the youngest of the apostles, perhaps a late teenager when first meeting the Master, he was anything but effeminate. Rather he was full of spunk and spirit.

In fact, Jesus called John and his brother James "sons of Boanerges" or "sons of thunder" (Mark 3:17). Their volcanic characters were displayed when they wanted to call down fire on the Samaritan village for denying hospitality to their Master. Also, they possessed inordinate ambition, petitioning Jesus for the two top positions in His coming kingdom. As we saw in the previous chapter, the Master rebuked both their vengeful zeal and unholy aspiration. But three years in His presence and under His training tamed these children of the storm, transforming their thunder into tenderness.

## John's Early Life

More boys round the world have been named for the Apostle John than for any other Bible character. A survey a few years ago counted roughly 6 million boys in America bearing the name *John*. Of the apostles' names, James was next popular with about 3 million. Thomas followed with approximately 2 million, then Peter with a third of a million.

With his brother James, John was a partner with Andrew and Peter in a fishing business in Capernaum. His father was Zebedee (Matt. 10:2). Fishing was rugged labor, demanding and developing hard muscles. Rowing through heavy waves resulted in calloused hands. Mending the nets, as they dried on racks under sunny skies, bronzed the lean form of this manly youth.

John, along with Andrew, was directed to Jesus by John the Baptist. After an interview with Jesus, John was convinced that He was the long-promised Messiah. So memorable was the conversation that 60 years later John recalled the time as the 10th hour of the day (John 1:35-39). From that moment on Jesus was the light of John's life. The affection was mutual. John is described as "the disciple whom Jesus loved." After that first meeting, John returned to his fishing but interrupted it for tours with Jesus. Then came the call to follow Jesus. Along with James,

Peter, and Andrew, he willingly left father, boats, fish, and business to become a fisher of men.

### John's Intolerance (Mark 9:38-40; Luke 9:49-50)

On a preaching mission in some village John noticed a crowd. He pushed forward to see what the commotion was all about. A demon-possessed boy was groaning on the ground, his head tossing from side to side. John thought of using his delegated authority to cast out the demon. But before he could act, a total stranger cast out the evil spirit. The boy gave a convulsive twist, grew silent, then later stood healed and calm.

That's when John the thunderer became unglued. Pushing forward, he confronted the startled healer in a loud voice, "How dare you use my Master's name! By what right do you do this sort of thing? You have no authorization from Him. I'm one of His inner circle, and I've never seen you before. I order you to stop using His name!"

When John reported this irregular, fraudulent worker, he may have expected some brownie points for his zeal. Instead, Jesus rebuked him for his bigotry. John highhandedly assumed that those outside Jesus' circle could in no way speak for Him or do works in His name. Recounted John, "Master, we saw one casting out devils in Thy name, and he followeth not us; and we forbade him, because he followeth not us" (Mark 9:38).

Jesus replied, "Forbid him not: for he that is not against us is for us" (Luke 9:50). Judging by John's report, Jesus knew that this healer was not a professional exorcist like the later seven sons of Sceva, who merely used Jesus' name as a magic word to gain money (Acts 19:13-14). Rather this was a sincere man whose heart had been somewhere influenced by the ministry of Jesus, and who wanted to emulate His service to needy people. Perhaps he even possessed spiritual gifts equal to those of the apostles.

John's bigotry was really an extension of his ambition to be top dog. His pride in being an apostle was showing. But Jesus said, "There is no man which shall do a miracle in My name, that can lightly speak evil of Me" (Mark 9:39). John was wrong to rule out one who, though not among the apostolic group, was doing the Master's work in the Master's name.

What a vivid lesson for believers who seek to deny the power of Christ in those who don't belong to their exclusive groups. In Christ there is room for *many* groups to follow—just so they follow Him.

Naturally, we cannot support the ministry of those who deny the fundamentals of the faith. In later years John warned strongly against endorsing the work of Christ-deniers. But within the limits of God's Word we need tolerant, forbearing spirits toward those who don't see theological issues exactly as we do. How dangerous to think that our denomination is the only true church. Because a group does not follow us precisely, whether Baptists, Methodists, Lutherans, Episcopalians, or Pentecostals, is no reason to exclude them.

John's spirit was the forerunner of that zeal that led John Huss and Savonarola to be burned at the stake. It also foreshadowed the intolerance of the Conventicle Act passed by the British Parliament in 1664 which "punished with fine, imprisonment and transportation on a third offense, all persons who met in greater numbers than five, for any act of dissenting worship, which met outside the established church." That spirit also presaged the Five Mile Act of 1665 which forbade expelled clergymen "under penalty of forty pounds and six months imprisonment, to approach within five miles of any corporate town, or borough, or of any parish in which they had previously taught or preached." Such narrowmindedness resulted in the jailing of John Bunyan for 12 years. John's spirit also pretyped the rigidity of those today who worship with only a select group of friends whose race, education, social status, opinions, politics, whims, hobbies, or dogma conform to their own.

Such diviseness wastes a lot of spiritual energy. When the English and French were at war in colonial Canada, Admiral Phipps, in charge of the British fleet, was ordered to anchor outside Quebec, a city on the St. Lawrence River. He was to wait the coming of British infantry and then join the land forces in attack. Arriving early, Admiral Phipps, an ardent nonconformist, was annoyed by the statues of the saints which adorned the roofs and towers of the Roman Catholic cathedral. So he spent his time shooting at them with the ships' guns. How many he hit we don't know. But history recorded that when the infantry arrived and the signal was given for attack, the Admiral found himself out of ammunition. He had used it for shooting at the saints.

Says the poet,

> He drew a circle and shut me out,
> Heretic, rebel, a thing to flout.
> But love and I had a will to win—
> We drew a circle and took him in!

The sovereign Spirit of unity dislikes fanatic sectarianism, unbiblical separationism, and unnecessary divisiveness.

## John's Transformation

A gardener asked a piece of fragrant clay in his garden, "How come you have such a sweet aroma?" Answered the clay, "Because they placed me near a rose."

Constant association with the Rose of Sharon transformed John from a quick-tempered youth to a man of gentleness. His ambitions decreased. His intolerance subsided. Under the training of Jesus, the fiery youth became a warmhearted man.

Evangelical scholars believe that John wrote not only the Gospel that bears his name, but also three epistles: 1, 2, and 3 John, as well as Revelation. About a century ago some liberal writers questioned John's authorship of the three epistles. They claimed there was a radical difference between the John of the Gospel and the John of the epistles. The fourth Gospel paints John as angry, ambitious, and intolerant, while the author of the epistles is the epitome of love. John had been transformed by the Master, changed from son of thunder to apostle of love. Beholding his Lord, as in a mirror, John conformed to His image.

It was a slow process. John never lost his volcanic potential, for it always slumbered beneath the surface of his personality.

But the overruling presence and power of the indwelling Christ directed his disruptive drives into tender channels. Many of our drives are neither good nor bad, but neutral—capable of being directed for bad uses or for God's glory. We shall see later that John's strong spirit firmly spoke out against false doctrine and iniquitous behavior.

John's change of disposition is an encouragement to us. Ornery, selfish, whining youths need not grow up into ornery, selfish, whining adults. Through the laws of spiritual growth, green bitter fruit can ripen into something luscious and lovely.

## John's Love Displayed

John's thunder-turned-tender character revealed itself in his loyalty and bravery at the cross and in the early days of the church. After fleeing in panic with the rest from Gethsemane, John was the first to rally. Though Peter followed afar off, John courageously entered the courtyard (John 18:15-16). Apparently he was known to the high priest, perhaps because of his father's business connections.

Through his influence, John got Peter inside the courtyard too. But while Peter lingered around the fire, justifiably afraid because of his attack on the high priest's servant, John apparently entered the trial room with Jesus during the interrogation (v. 15). While Peter issued his threefold denial, then left in bitter tears, John remained true.

Of all the apostles, John alone is mentioned as standing by the cross. He had the manliness to stand in the midst of Christ's enemies, while they spat out their venomous hate, and not run away.

John was the only apostle mentioned or addressed by Jesus in His seven last words from the cross. Looking at John, Jesus said to His mother, "Woman, behold thy son!" Then directing John to His mother, "Behold thy mother!" (John 19:26-27)

After taking Mary to his house in Jerusalem, John hurried back in time to hear Jesus' final sayings. Only John recorded, "I thirst," and "It is finished!" Then he saw Jesus bow His head and dismiss His spirit. John alone tells of the piercing of Jesus' side and the flow of blood and water, also of the burial by Nicodemus and Joseph (vv. 38-42). He was courageous and devoted to the end. Seeing the Lamb led to the slaughter, John became the preacher of the slain and resurrected Lamb.

Though Peter dominated the first half of Acts, John was his companion in most episodes. Their special friendship, probably begun as boys, had been strengthened by their business partnership. Impulsive Peter and spirited John made a great team. Likely they formed one of the pairs when Jesus sent His disciples out two by two. They were the two sent by the Master to prepare the Passover (Luke 22:8). They must have been staying together after the crucifixion, for they raced to the empty tomb together, youthful John outrunning Peter (John 20:4).

John went with Peter to the temple to pray. Though Peter was the spokesman, the record indicates both spoke to the crowd after the healing of the lame man. They were arrested and jailed together. They were tried before the Sanhedrin who saw the boldness of John as well as of Peter. Told not to speak nor teach any more in the name of Jesus, John joined Peter in answering, "We cannot but speak the things which we have seen and heard (Acts 4:20; see also Acts 3—4).

When Samaritans began to believe the Gospel through the ministry of Philip, John and Peter went down to investigate (Acts 8:14). Though John appears no more in Acts, Paul wrote that on a visit to Jerusalem he found John, one of the pillars of the Jerusalem church, along with Peter and James, the brother of Jesus (Gal. 2:9). How wonderful to see these two friends evangelizing together, facing opposition together, compelled by common love for their Master.

## Mutual Love of Jesus and John

Jesus seemed closer to some apostles than to others. An increasing degree of intimacy which His followers enjoyed in relationship to Him may be traced from the larger groups to the more exclusive. On the outer fringe were the 500 brethren (1 Cor. 15:6), then the 120 (Acts 1:15), then the 70 (Luke 10:1), then the Twelve, then the inner three, then finally the beloved John, so often called "the disciple whom Jesus loved" (John 13:23; 20:2; 21:7, 20). John certainly lived up to his name which means, "favored of Jehovah."

Apparently, John was not only one of the inner three, but he was the only one described as the disciple whom Jesus loved, and he was given the position closest to Christ in the Upper Room (John 13:23). In early church literature John is sometimes called, "The Epistethios," meaning the one who reclined on Jesus' bosom. In giving directions about the care of His mother, John was the last friend to whom Jesus spoke before He died.

John became the apostle of love. He gave us the famous, "For God so loved the world" (John 3:16). He reminded us of Christ's new commandment to love one another, not only as a duty, but as a badge of discipleship, "as I have loved you, that ye also love one another. By this shall all men know that ye are My disciples, if ye have love one to another" (13:34-35). John referred to love over 50 times in his writings.

Jesus promised spiritual insight to those who show their love through obedience. "He that hath My commandments, and keepeth them, he it is that loveth Me; and he that loveth Me shall be loved of My Father, and I will love him, and will manifest Myself to him" (14:21). The beloved John was given an amazing grasp of spiritual truth, including the apocalyptic visions of Revelation. John may have been the first of the disciples to believe the Resurrection, and after fishing all night was the first to recognize Jesus on the shore (John 20:8; 21:7).

Of all four Gospels, John gave us the loftiest conception of Christ. Whereas the other Gospel writers present the outer history of Jesus, John's portrait penetrates to the holy of holies of Jesus' radiant personality. Some regard the Gospel of John as the most profound book of all time, the supreme literary work of the world. Nearly half the verses in John are the words of our Lord.

Out of all the wonders which Jesus performed, John recorded miracles which would convince his readers that Jesus was the Christ, the very Son of God (20:30-31). Whereas Matthew presented Christ as King, Mark presented him as the Servant, and Luke viewed Him as an Ideal Man, John soared eagle-high to depict Christ's unclouded glory and to prove His exalted claims.

Through the centuries many have become convinced of Christ's deity by the beauty and power of John's Gospel. In a high school class a Christian boy witnessed to his faith. His skeptical teacher suggested a debate between this believer and an unbeliever in the class on the subject *Is the Bible the Word of God?* The teacher was careful to pick a clever debater as the Christian's opponent.

When the time came for the debate, the Christian boy just quoted a few verses from the Bible. Then the second boy rose to speak. "I have never read much of the Bible before. As I prepared, I thought that if I were to debate on this topic, I should at least read some of the Bible. I want you to know that I have read the Gospel of John through, not once, but five times. I also want you to know that I have come to the conclusion that Jesus is the Son of God. Also, I have come to believe on Him for eternal life."

After reading John, many with doubts about the deity of Christ have had their doubts dissolve into sure conviction that Jesus is God. If you have doubts, I challenge you to read the Gospel of John through two or three times with an open mind, asking God to show you His truth.

## John's Love Was Tough

Though John epitomized love, it was love with backbone. True love can be tough, warding off all that would injure the object of its affection. Just as a loving father would protect his toddling youngster against a vicious dog, so John warned against popular false teaching aimed right at the vitals of his "little children."

He did not hesitate to call those whose walk contradicted their talk liars (1 John 1:6; 2:4). He forbade believers to welcome into their homes, or endorse in any way, those who held false views of Christ (2 John 10). He exposed Diotrophes for his dictatorial assumptions and malicious words (3 John 9-10). John didn't lose his tendency to thunder, but his denunciation was restrained with humility and charity.

Irenaeus, bishop of Lyon and distinguished early church theologian, reported that John penned some of his writings to refute the errors of gnosticism, a philosophy which held that matter was essentially evil. Therefore to explain creation while holding to a holy God, Gnostics believed in a series of intermediate, subordinate emanations from God, too far removed to contaminate deity, yet with power sufficient to create. This helps us to see why John began his Gospel, "In the beginning was the Word, and the Word was with God, and the Word was God . . . All things were made by Him; and without Him was not anything made that was made" (John 1:1, 3).

Since matter was evil, Gnostics denied the real humanity of Christ, distinguishing between the man Jesus and the ageless Christ who came on Jesus at His baptism and left Him on the cross. To combat this error of a phantom Second Person of the Trinity, John wrote, "That which we have heard, which we have seen with our eyes, which we have looked upon, and our hands have handled of the Word of life: For this life was manifested, and we have seen it" (1 John 1:1-2). We also comprehend John's insistence on the truth "that Jesus Christ is come in the flesh" (4:2).

Because of its downgrading of the body, some Gnostics taught that the sins of the flesh did not affect the soul, thus promoting sinful living. John's repeated warnings against the practices of sin were directed against this Gnostic heresy.

One graphic legend tells how John, visiting a public bath in Ephesus, caught a glimpse of Cerinthus, champion of Gnosticism, inside. Immediately John rushed out of the bathhouse without bathing, exclaiming, "Let us flee, lest even the bathhouse fall down because Cerinthus, the enemy of truth, is within."

On another occasion John reputedly called Cerinthus, "the firstborn of the devil." Though probably apocryphal, these stories do reflect the presence of that thunderous nature, for many decades under the control of the Master, now evidencing itself with proper constraint. Tender but tough.

Contrary to the idea that scholarly use of the mind dulls the warmness of the heart, John's love was not dimmed by his keenness of intellect. Loving God with his mind, he wrote five books. His Gospel's prologue, a deeply philosophical treatise on

Christ as the Logos, earned for him the title of "Christian Plato." The church fathers of the third century attached to his name as author of Revelation the title "The Divine," literally, "The Theologian."

As stated earlier, liberal scholars have tried to say a different John wrote 1 John. Yet even the casual reader must be struck with the similarity of language between the Gospel and the epistle. Both use such words as *beginning, Word, life, light, darkness, witness, walk, know, true, confess, children of God, sin, propitiation, love, boldness, flesh, believe,* and *Paraclete.* Wouldn't this point to a common author?

Interestingly, in his Gospel John modestly keeps himself in the background. In fact, he never mentions himself once by name, not even when listing the apostles, whereas Matthew, Mark, and Luke mention his name about 30 times. Five times he refers to himself as the disciple whom Jesus loved, three times to *that, other,* or *another* disciple, but never to *John.* Such a retiring, reticent disposition is a far cry from the brash youth who asked Jesus for top honor in the kingdom. Though John had a keen mind, he reveled in the fact that Jesus loved him. Someone has said that in the fourth Gospel, John is never visible, and Jesus is never invisible.

## John's Final Years

Irenaeus, a native of Asia Minor, who knew Polycarp, a disciple of John, claims John lived at Ephesus till the time of Trajan, who became emperor in A.D. 98. On a visit to Ephesus, I was shown the "House of St. Mary" where the mother of Jesus supposedly lived under John's care. Two traditional sites exist for John's tomb.

Tradition says an attempt was made to poison John, but God spared him. This is why the symbol for John is a chalice with a snake issuing from it. Another legend says that during a persecution he was thrown into a cauldron of boiling water but emerged unharmed.

We do know that John was exiled to Patmos, a small ruggedly beautiful but lonely island penal colony in the Aegean Sea not far from Ephesus. John wrote in the salutation of Revelation, "I John, who also am your brother and companion in tribulation, and in the kingdom and patience of Jesus Christ, was in the isle that is called Patmos, for the Word of God and for the testimony of Jesus Christ" (Rev. 1:9). Banished there by Emperor Domitian, he received the message and visions of the last book of the Bible. John's heart was gladdened by a glimpse of the ultimate victory of martyrs and saints, and of the divine, brighter side to persecution. In the final chapter he wrote, "I John saw these things, and heard them" (22:8).

Apparently Emperor Trajan allowed John to leave Patmos and return to Ephesus. We learn from 2 and 3 John that his concern for the missionary work of his followers in Asia Minor carried through to the close of his life. He delighted to hear that his spiritual children were walking in the truth. He warned them to take care lest they lose their full reward. He noted the good deeds of Gaius and Demetrius, and likewise the arrogance of Diotrophes. He wished to go and speak to his spiritual children face to face.

John's life compassed a great span. A lad when he first followed Christ, he lived the longest of the Twelve. He died around A.D. 100 having lived into his 90s. Paradoxically, his brother James was the first of the apostles to die.

John could teach us much about growing old gracefully. Early in life he submitted to the power of Christ's love which progressively cooled his youthful hotheadedness. To be a loving, gracious person at 60 or 80, we must start earlier to yield to the influence of Christ.

Gustave Dore was putting the finishing touches on the face of Christ in one of his paintings. A friend said, "You must love Him very much to be able to paint Him like that."

"Love Him, madam?" exclaimed Dore. "I do love Him, but if I loved Him better I could paint Him better."

We need to pray "more love to Thee, O Christ." Then that love, shed abroad in our hearts, will flow to those around us.

# 6

# Philip, the Cautious

A church board was discussing the need for a new church auditorium. Growing attendances crowded out the small sanctuary for both morning services. The evening service was also an overflow. The church met its bills easily. A preliminary report unanimously recommended building a new sanctuary.

A board member known for his conservatism spoke up, "Gentlemen, where will we get the money? We don't have a large building fund. Shouldn't we wait till we have most of the money in the bank? Let's not move too fast."

The discussion continued nearly two hours as members graciously and freely weighed the pros and cons. At the end a large majority urged stepping out on faith, so voted to form a building committee. Three years later the congregation was worshiping in a beautiful new sanctuary. The mortgage payments were easily met week by week.

The cautious board member reminds me of the Apostle Philip. Philip had to have things down in black and white. His analytical mind needed to mull over the facts, weighing the pros and cons scrupulously. In fact, Philip kept so within the boundaries of careful calculation that he sometimes was indecisive and dependent on others for help. He was never guilty of snap judgments.

Philip means "lover of horses." Perhaps he was named after Philip of Macedon whose son, Alexander the Great, left a lasting Greek influence in northern Galilee. Or maybe he received his name in honor of a local ruler, Philip the Tetrarch, who had honored the apostle's hometown, Bethsaida, by raising it to the rank of a city. With Greek influence in his background, Philip could be useful to the Master who would want His message taken to Greeks as well as Jews.

Since Bethsaida was also the hometown of Andrew and Peter, Philip may have enjoyed their friendship from his earliest days (John 1:44). His parental name is not known. Likely he was a fisherman, since fishing was the chief industry of that area. He shared the interest of Andrew and Peter in their search for the Messiah. This ultimately led him to charter membership in "the world's most famous fishing club."

Philip's temperament differed radically from that of his longtime friend, Peter. The night Peter ventured to walk on water, Philip was probably reasoning to himself, "Everyone knows water is a liquid, not a solid. Try to walk on it, and you'll sink." Unlike Peter who would step out on faith, Philip leaned more on his other longtime friend, Andrew, in moments of indecision.

Philip, the apostle, should not be confused with Philip, the deacon, who dispensed alms in the early church and led a successful missionary crusade in Samaria. Philip the deacon also explained the Gospel to the Ethiopian eunuch and was the only person called an "evangelist" in the New Testament. He had four daughters who prophesied, and he entertained Paul on his return journey to Jerusalem (Acts 6:5; 8:12, 26-40; 21:8-9).

What we do know about the Apostle Philip we find in the Gospel of John. Let's look at four episodes that depict Philip's character.

## Prudent in His Witness to Nathanael (John 1:43-46)

Philip belonged to that group (e.g., Andrew, Peter, James, and John) who were looking for the Messiah's coming. Together, with another close friend, Nathanael, Philip had researched the Old Testament promises concerning the consolation of Israel.

After recording Andrew's bringing Peter to Jesus, the Gospel says, "The day following Jesus would go forth into Galilee, and findeth Philip, and saith unto him, 'Follow Me' " (John 1:43). It may well be that Andrew and Peter had told Philip about Jesus. Somewhere along the route between Bethany and Galilee, Jesus invited Philip to become one of His followers. Jesus did not stumble on Philip accidentally, but deliberately enlisted him, perhaps having been acquainted with him as a follower of John the Baptist.

Note that Jesus found Philip. The Good Shepherd went after the sheep. What was true here is equally true in every genuine conversion. Our seeking of Him is really the reflex action of His first seeking us. For example, though it looked like the tax collector Zacchaeus was seeking Jesus, even climbing a tree to glimpse Him, yet Zacchaeus merely sought to see what Jesus looked like, with no intention of stopping Him. It was Jesus who stopped, looked up into the tree, and invited Himself to Zacchaeus' house. Jesus' comment at the end of the story tells who really did the seeking, "For the Son of man is come to seek and to save that which was lost" (Luke 19:10).

Philip responded affirmatively to Jesus' call. Interestingly, tradition identifies Philip with the man who answered, "Suffer me first to go and bury my father" (Matt. 8:21). If that is true, it would fit his trait of indecisiveness. But if Philip *did* delay, it was not for long. Looking into the eyes of Jesus and hearing His voice, Philip knew his life would never be the same. He began to follow. Though Philip's choices were often slowly deliberated, they were deep and ultimate.

Then Philip remembered his buddy, Nathanael. Immediately he hurried to tell him. This was Philip's first act of evangelism. Out of gratitude for his newfound life, and with genuine missionary spirit he shared the Good News with his close friend.

Philip told Nathanael, "We have found Him, of whom Moses in the Law, and the Prophets, did write, Jesus of Nazareth, the son of Joseph" (John 1:45).

At that point, Philip was convinced that Jesus was the fulfillment of the law and prophets. But when he expressed his conviction to Nathanael, he ran into a road block. Nathanael asked, "Can any good thing come out of Nazareth?" (v. 46, NASB), implying that Jerusalem would be a more logical place.

Philip could have resented his friend's refusal to accept his testimony. Or he could have listed all the Old Testament predictions fulfilled in Jesus. But refusing to argue, he simply answered, "Come and see" (v. 46). Though reasoned dialogue may lay a good foundation for faith, we cannot argue anyone into the kingdom.

Perhaps we are giving Philip too much credit for his approach. Possibly Philip's reaction to Nathanael's objection did not stem from wise soul-winning methodology, but rather from feelings of inadequacy. Conscious of his limitations in argument, he referred his friend to Jesus. This explanation fits Philip's personality trait as lacking positiveness, often unsure of his ground.

Such dependence on the Lord is not a bad idea for a person who feels over his head in witness or discussion. He would be wise to say, "I'm not able to answer all your questions. But I can introduce you to Someone who has answers. I invite you to come to church this Sunday morning. I'll pick you up at 10 A.M."

Philip's strategy paid off. Nathanael was convinced of Jesus' Messiahship. With Andrew, John, and Peter already converted (and probably James around this time too), it's not surprising Philip is listed fifth, and Nathanael sixth, in all three Gospels (Matt. 10:3; Mark 3:18; Luke 6:14). When the apostles went out later two by two, Philip and Nathanael were probably paired off.

### **Practicality in Feeding the 5,000** (John 6:5-14)

Around 1900 a pastor in Dayton, Ohio read an article prophesying that human beings would one day fly. The article was illustrated with sketches of a flying machine drawn by Leonardo da Vinci. The pastor, indignant that men would try to do what God obviously had not intended, spent the next several years trying to prove that men neither could nor would ever fly. At the same time two Dayton boys went to work on the opposite assumption. Today an airport in Dayton is named for the Wright brothers, but no one remembers the pastor's name. Someone dubbed the pastor, "Philip," because the apostle who bore that name seemed good at cataloging obstacles instead of finding solutions. The story of the feeding of the 5,000 is a case in point.

*Philip calculated.* One day when Jesus saw thousands of people following Him, He said to Philip, "Whence shall we buy bread, that these may eat?" He knew what He was going to do, but asked this question to prove Philip, who didn't pass the test.

Philip pressed a few buttons on his mental computer. With some tidy, practical division he figured that the crowd would require over 200 denarii worth of bread. This irreducible minimum would give everyone just a little. Since a denarius was a workman's pay for one day, Philip replied something like, "It'll take nearly a year's pay to buy enough to give this mob a bite each! Besides if we did have the money, how could we get the food here on such short notice?"

His precise logical mind had it all figured out in terms of need. His modern counterpart might be a dapperly dressed man shopping in the supermarket, pushing his cart with his list in hand, jotting down the price of each item as he takes it from the shelf, and making sure at the checkout that the cashier's total agrees with his. He takes the groceries to a shiny spic-and-span car. Driving home, he never takes a chance. In fact, he's so cautious other drivers often honk at him. His driveway leads to a clean garage beside a well-manicured lawn. He never misses the 10 P.M. news and goes to bed immediately thereafter. When he serves on the church board, he is always prompt and predictable. And pragmatic. Methodical, mathematical, and almost mechanical, he is forever reviewing traditions, investigating foundations, and adding figures. He often says, "We've never done it that way before." Or, "It can't be done."

Modern Philips can impede God's work. One influential board member prevented a growing Sunday School from constructing a badly needed educational building. He argued, "We've just gotten the church out of debt. I'd never vote for assuming another obligation as long as I'm on the board. Let's use common sense."

*Philip calculated without faith.* Philip was a man of limited vision. Depending solely on proofs, computation, and bottom lines, he forgot the Lord was ready to meet any emergency. Philip never thought of divine power to feed the thousands; to him it was a matter of dollars and cents. His temperament ruled out the miraculous. He knew too much arithmetic to be adventurous.

To help train Philip in the school of faith, Jesus asked him about bread for the crowd. When Philip gave his unimaginative answer, the Master then turned to Andrew who was standing there with a boy with a lunch basket. Andrew's remark contrasted refreshingly with Philip's lack of vision. "There is a lad here, which hath five barley loaves, and two small fishes; but what are they among so many?" (John 6:9) In response to Andrew's faith, however embryonic, Jesus multiplied the boy's lunch sufficiently to feed the whole crowd with 12 basketfuls left over.

*Hopefully, Philip learned to include God in his calculations thereafter.* Philip must have been shamed to the depths of his soul. "I should have known. He who can still the storm, heal the sick, and change water into wine can feed the multitude. Why didn't I say, 'Lord, feeding this crowd is no problem for You.' Why didn't I have faith?"

Philip learned something that day about his own wooden, uncreative earthiness. But he also learned that little is much if God is in it.

The church needs prudent leaders to safeguard against presumptious, harebrained, budget-breaking ideas. But the church also needs men of faith to see greater ministries accomplished. Without faith there would have been no Mayflower, no church among the Auca Indians.

A calculating, conservative head doesn't necessarily indicate a cold heart. Nor does thoroughness of research automatically indicate unbelief. Philip, a man with a logical mind, probably had a warm heart that very much wanted to feed the crowd, but didn't see how it could be done. He needed to exchange his sense of the impossible for a sense of the possible through God.

Too often we figure without God. When the Israelites came to the Red Sea, hemmed in on both sides, pursued by the Egyptians, things looked impossible. "But God" parted the waters to bring them safely through (Ex. 14:8-31). When imprisoned Peter was scheduled for execution in the morning, it seemed everything was over for him. "But God" knocked off his chains and opened the prison gate to free him (Acts 12:1-10). Things may look impossible for us, "but God" is able. The Lord must be taken into our calculations.

**Indecision in Welcoming the Greeks** (John 12:19-22)
After the raising of Lazarus, the Pharisees complained that "the world is gone after Him" (John 12:19). Then to show how widely His fame had circulated, John added, "And there were certain Greeks among them that came up to worship at the feast" (v. 20). These Greek Passover pilgrims were earnest seekers, descendents of Socrates, Plato, and Aristotle, many of whose utterances were really one long heart cry for truth.

On the outskirts of the crowd listening to this illustrious Teacher, they decided they wanted to interview Him. But how? Through one of His followers, but which one? They chose Philip. Was it because Philip bore a Greek name? Or were they acquainted with him previously, since they came from Bethsaida, Philip's home town? The Greeks approached Philip, requesting, "Sir, we would see Jesus" (v. 21).

But Philip did not take them directly to Jesus. He had to think it over. What bothered him was that these men were not Jews. Had not Jesus once told them to "go rather to the lost sheep of the house of Israel"? (Matt. 10:6) These visitors were aliens, foreigners, Gentiles, one step below the Samaritans. *Would Jesus want me to bring them?* Philip argued within.

Philip seems to have been reluctant to act on his own initiative. Not sure if it was a good idea to give these outsiders access to the Master, he turned to consult good old Andrew. "After all, Andrew, we have to be careful. We can't act too quickly. Do you think Jesus would approve?" It was one thing to bring Nathanael, a Jew, to his Master, but another thing to introduce Gentiles.

With Andrew there was no hesitation. He may have said to Philip, "Don't you know the Master better than that? He never sends people away. Remember the Syro-Phoenician woman? And the Samaritans? And now the Greeks. Hasn't He talked about God loving the whole world? This could be a real encouragement to Him!"

Philip, slow but not stubborn, accompanied Andrew to tell Jesus. The record implies that the Master spoke with these Greeks. They heard some marvelous teaching including, "He that loveth his life shall lose it; and he that hateth his life in this world shall keep it unto life eternal. . . . And I, if I be lifted up from the earth, will draw all men unto Me" (John 12:25, 32).

Philip's analytical spirit might never have set Galilee or Jerusalem on fire, but his willingness to be led in the proper direction kindled a fire in his own heart. Perhaps Philip was aware of his insecurity and his need for seeking a second opinion. Through association with the Lord Jesus Christ and the indwelling of the Holy Spirit, Philip doubtless made great strides in overcoming his limitations. The over prudent matured into greater decisiveness.

It's possible to delay too long in making up our minds. What if Philip had continued to hem and haw? The Greeks might have gone on their way, never to meet Jesus. Some believers dillydally reluctantly in the face of major opportunities. Philip should have welcomed the Greeks with open arms, hurrying them toward Jesus.

A suburban church was approached by an evangelical group of another culture who wished to use a room for their service on the off-hour Sunday afternoons. When the board took too long to consider if their people would like a "foreign" element holding regular meetings in their lovely building, the "strangers" went elsewhere where a warm welcome was granted them.

Visitors to some churches receive a cool welcome, if any at all. These outsiders seem to say, "We would see Jesus," but the repelling glances seem to reply, "What are you doing in our lovely building? *We* paid for it." The visitors wait for some word of invitation, some hint that the insiders would like to help them. Don't leave the invitation to Andrew.

**Slowness in Seeing the Father** (John 14:8-11)
After Jesus made the marvelous declaration that He was the only way to the Father, He added, "If ye had known Me, ye should have known My Father also: and from henceforth ye know Him, and have seen Him" (v. 7).

To Philip's rational, analytical mind, the Father was some far-off, hazy blur. So he said, "Lord, show us the Father, and it sufficeth us" (v. 8).

In itself this request seems devout. Yet in other respects Philip's desire was defective. First, he expressed the crude notion that the Father could appear in physical form, externalized as an outward visible object. Second, that a mere objective vision of the Father would "suffice" to reveal all the wonder of His being. And third, Philip's petition revealed how little he (and the others) had gained from their three years with Jesus. Three years with Him—and they had not seen His glory beyond the seamless robe. Jesus had taught so much about God, and yet it was still a mystery. Philip's common-sense mind was still very much in a fog. So he asked to see the Father.

Disappointed, but characteristically patient with His slow, earthbound disciple, Jesus answered, "Have I been so long time with you, and yet has thou not known Me, Philip? He that hath seen Me hath seen the Father; and how sayest thou then, 'Show us the Father'? Believest thou not that I am in the Father, and the Father in Me? The words that I speak unto you I speak not of Myself: but the Father that dwelleth in Me, He doeth the works" (vv. 9-10).

In other words, Philip, "You've been so cautious, too practical. Have you not seen Me at work? Recall how I fed the multitudes and healed the sick. When you heard My words or saw My miracles, you were hearing and seeing the Father."

We are certainly indebted to Philip for his question, for Jesus' answer contains the central affirmation of the Christian faith—namely, that Jesus is God. In Jesus, God is at work. In Jesus, God's plans for His children are revealed. To follow Jesus' example is to walk God's way.

Philip was a man for whom faith was difficult. Though slow

to apprehend, he kept inquiring diligently into spiritual reality. He began to unbottle his rational mind and take his questions to Jesus. Philip found in Him all he looked for and needed. For our age of scientific approach, rationalism, and pragmatism when so many Philips are demanding proof, it is Jesus Christ who supplies the practical, down-to-earth answers. The Lord wants us to look beyond our own limited resources to His infinite power and presence.

When Ralph and Carolyn Partelow felt called to leave their 10-year pastorate in Pennsylvania in early 1977 and apply for the mission field, the idea scared them half to death. Knowing he needed more training, Ralph asked, "How will I ever pay for an education, much less life? For us to ever get to the mission field will take a miracle."

They decided, if things fell into place, to enroll in the Alliance School of Theology and Missions at Nyack, New York. They would need a ground-floor apartment because of Carolyn's multiple sclerosis. They would also need a place where Ralph could have a workshop because he expected to support himself and his wife by making miniature pianos, a hobby of his. And they would need people sending in orders for these miniatures. To their astonishment, all these conditions were met.

Ralph resigned from his pastorate in mid-May. The next few months, before the beginning of the fall semester, sufficient orders came in to provide life's necessities plus his education.

The Partelows were no strangers to God's wonder-working ability. Earlier in their marriage, when tests revealed Carolyn had MS, she was also told she could never have children. Then she gave birth to Jonathan, a lively son.

After school started in September a fellow-student who worked for the Africa Inland Mission mentioned that his mission field might interest the Partelows. Ralph and Carolyn had already been rejected by three other mission boards because of Carolyn's health, but they went for an interview. To their surprise the mission was indeed interested.

In January 1978 the Partelows were officially accepted by the Africa Inland Mission, but learned that they had to have thousands of dollars worth of equipment before their departure in 12 months. By human computation the task was impossible. Ralph wondered if there were still people who would buy his pianos—enough people to raise the money he needed. The night of his acceptance by the AIM, orders totaling over $3,000 came in by phone. *God is telling me that nothing is too hard for Him,* Ralph thought.

Incredibly, the following month he received orders for nearly 150 instruments, and more orders kept coming in till he had to establish a cutoff date in order to fill all orders before leaving for the mission field. Partelow's miniatures were so well done that he was written up in the *New York Times* and *Miniature Collector.*

The Partelows had a fruitful ministry in Kenya for over a year in a climate amenable to Carolyn's illness. When her condition worsened in 1980, they returned to America where Ralph pastored two small upstate New York churches. With Carolyn's health improving remarkably, they returned to missionary work in Africa in the summer of 1981.

The Partelow's faith sets a good example for us. We must always look beyond the narrow bounds of our limited vision to the vast vista of God's unrestricted territory.

# 7

# Bartholomew—Nathanael, the Guileless

The well-known author, Madeleine L'Engle, has her "special place," a secret hideout near her New England home. A 10-minute walk beyond her lawn, past a willow tree, across a pasture, then over a stone wall, brings her to a brook where a natural stone bridge enables her to dangle her legs in the water. If she sits for a while, gazing at foliage and sky reflected in the water, her tensions and frustrations gradually ease.

Nathanael had his quiet spot too. Jesus spoke of seeing him "under the fig tree" (John 1:48). For many in Galilee in the first century the fig tree was a sort of private room. Growing to an approximate height of 15 feet, the tree spread its branches outward to 25 feet. Since many houses had only one room, those who wanted solitude sought privacy under the shade of the fig tree.

This disciple has two names: Bartholomew and Nathanael. *Bar* means "son of." Imaginatively the second part of his name has been linked with Talmai, a king whose daughter married David and mothered Absalom (2 Sam. 3:3). Others connect the second part of his name with Ptolemy, king of Egypt. Both suggestions make Bartholomew of royal lineage, but are highly unlikely.

His second name, Nathanael, means "gift of God," and as in the case of other disciples, may have been given by Jesus.

Why do we consider Bartholomew and Nathanael to be the same person? The first three Gospels and Acts all list Bartholomew sixth or seventh in the list of the Twelve (Matt. 10:3; Mark 3:18; Luke 6:14; Acts 1:13), but never mention Nathanael. The Gospel of John never mentions Bartholomew, but includes Nathanael in the company of the apostles, devoting seven verses to him in chapter 1, (vv. 45-51) and in the last chapter assuming him an apostle who came from Cana in Galilee, probably a fisherman (21:2). If Bartholomew and Nathanael are both names within the circle of the Twelve, by process of elimination they must refer to the same person.

The clinching argument is the close association of Bartholomew-Nathanael with Philip. In three listings Bartholomew is always paired with Philip. Then in John's account, it is Philip who brings Nathanael to Jesus. Bartholomew-Nathanael was Philip's friend.

Tradition says that Nathanael preached the Gospel in Phrygia, Hierapolis, and Armenia, perhaps even in India. One legend says he met his death beaten with clubs, flayed alive, and crucified head downward. His body was then tied up in a sack and tossed into the sea. Because he was supposedly flayed alive with knives, his apostolic symbol is usually three parallel knives, though sometimes it's the fig tree.

## Nathanael Searched the Scriptures

When Jesus told Nathanael that He saw him under the fig tree, He said in effect, "I saw you at study and prayer and meditation in your private quiet spot." Nathanael's friends knew that if he wasn't in his boat, they'd find him in his garden.

*Meditation*. Jesus knew Nathanael was a man of devotion. He knew this guileless soul was in the habit of spending many hours under the fig tree. In this quiet retreat Nathanael's spirit was refreshed and his character was strengthened.

We live in an age of noise. Teenagers have their radios blaring or their records blasting. Adults flick on the TV when entering their homes.

We also live in an age of hurry. Someone said, "What America needs is fewer 70-mile-an-hour sports cars and more rocking chairs." Or, to put it in the idiom of Nathanael's day, what we need is more fig trees.

Everyone should have a special place to ponder and pray. Isaac went into the fields at nighttime. Elijah communed with God in a cave. Jesus had Gethsemane. In his *Confessions*, Augustine graphically related how after evading communion with God for a long time, and arrested by the hand of God, he sought the secret place. "I cast myself under a certain fig tree. I know not how; and gave full vent to my tears, and floods broke forth from mine eyes, 'an acceptable sacrifice unto Thee!' "

*Prayer*. The shade of the fig tree was Nathanael's place of prayer. Prayer, the mightiest force in the universe, can bring us into union with God and release His power into a desperate world. Sadly, too many Christians fail to avail themselves of this power.

For a down-to-earth systematic prayer life, we need something to pray about and a quiet place to offer uninterrupted prayer. As for prayer content, the *Change the World School of Prayer* suggests a daily 15-minute period broken into three 5-minute segments. The first 5-minute section can be given to the worship of God. The second, to pray for needs that are close like family, friends, church, and community. The final segment, to pray for specific countries and missionaries.

Though the place of prayer may be any spot in the house allowing privacy, some families set aside a closet or spare room. One family saved the money to put down an inexpensive piece of carpet and to panel the walls of their prayer nook, so the atmosphere would be conducive to quiet intercession. Another family built a special little chapel in their backyard where members could go individually or together for prayer and devotions.

*Bible Study*. Nathanael did more than meditate and pray. He searched the Old Testament for the promise of the Messiah. He was well versed in the Scriptures. After Philip met the Lord, he found Nathanael and told him, "We have found Him, of whom Moses in the Law, and the Prophets, did write, Jesus of Nazareth, the son of Joseph" (John 1:45). Philip's phrasing seems to imply that the two of them had spent long hours pouring through the Law and the Prophets in search of information on the Messiah.

When Philip went looking for Nathanael, perhaps he first looked for him in his house, but found him under his fig tree with some portion of the Old Testament across his lap, pondering the advent of the Messiah. Like Nathanael, we need to be students of the Word.

Yet gross ignorance of Scripture prevails today. A test on Bible knowledge was given to 150 freshmen in a church college. Answers were startling. Some replied that the Ten Commandments were given by Jesus from the Mount of Olives. Others said Jesus was born in Rome, his mother's name was Gabriel, and He was baptized at Pentecost by John the Baptist in the Red Sea. Jesus died at Bethlehem after being betrayed by Samson.

Unfortunately, those college students aren't the only ones who don't know the Bible well. Even those who do read the Bible may study only from isolated parts—like the 23rd Psalm, the story of the Good Samaritan, or the love chapter (1 Cor. 13).

Since the Bible is the world's best-seller, we should read it out of sheer curiosity. We should also read it for its literary value and for the help it gives us in understanding much of our culture.

But the greatest reason for reading the Bible is because it speaks of the Mediator-Redeemer through whom we can be right with God. Jesus said, "Search the Scriptures . . . they are they which testify of Me" (John 5:39). Like Simeon and Anna, Nathanael believed in the Messianic promises. He was looking for the Christ, and thus was able to recognize the Son of God when He came.

## Nathanael Acknowledged His Skepticism

To Philip's eager announcement of finding the Messiah, Nathanael questioned, "Can there any good thing come out of Nazareth?" (John 1:46)

From his study of the Scriptures, Nathanael didn't expect the Messiah to come from Nazareth. Wouldn't the great Conqueror come clothed in royalty from Jerusalem, the capital? Or maybe from Bethlehem, which the Prophet Micah had predicted would be His birthplace? Perhaps it wasn't till Jesus' post-resurrection, Upper-Room explanation of the Old Testament prophecies that Nathanael and the other disciples understood Jesus' Nazarene background (Matt. 2:23; Luke 24:44-48).

Incidentally, it's possible for non-Christians to feel the same about the church. Observing inconsistencies among professing Christians—dishonesty, cruelty, and immorality—unbelievers candidly ask, "Can anything good come out of the church?" In reality, it's a caricature of Christ that prejudices them against genuine Christianity.

But Nathanael was honest in his skepticism. His study hadn't given him the slightest inkling that the Messiah would come from Nazareth. Likewise many people are biased against Christianity because of their inadequate understanding of the Bible. Either they have failed to read the Scriptures much or to interpret them correctly. They are sincere in their unbelief.

Honest skepticism opens the way to light and truth. A couple of years after Nathanael had made his remark, Jesus' enemies said, "Search, and look: for out of Galilee ariseth no prophet" (John 7:52). Their prejudice blinded them to His majesty and claims, leading them to reject Him. On the other hand, Nathanael's guileless skepticism opened the way for more investigation and light. His openness evidence moral integrity.

When Philip heard Nathanael's objection to the Messiah's Nazareth origin, he didn't waste time arguing. Brushing the remark aside, he merely answered, "Come and see" (1:46).

Nathanael was willing to investigate. After all, this "Messiah" had convinced Philip, his closest friend. The guileless heart does want to come and see. So Nathanael got moving.

## Nathanael's Grand Discovery

The two men walked back to the place Philip had left Jesus, perhaps at the village square. Philip was anxious. Nathanael was moderately excited, and due for a big surprise. The record says, "Jesus saw Nathanael coming to Him, and saith of him, 'Behold an Israelite indeed, in whom is no guile!' " (John 1:47) Nathanael's character was laid bare in one sentence.

*An Israelite Indeed.* Paul taught there were two kinds of seed in Israel, the children of the flesh and the children of the promise (Rom. 9:6-8). The natural seed did not possess the same spiritual faith as did their forefathers who walked in the faith of Abraham, and who before Christ's coming looked eagerly for the Messiah's coming. Jesus designated Nathanael as belonging to the spiritual seed. "Behold—an Israelite indeed," not in name or flesh only, but spiritually alive to God, a genuine believer, a type of God's intent for all Israel.

How wonderful when it is said of professing Christians today, "Not just baptized, not merely a church member, but a genuine born-again believer."

*In whom is no guile.* Quite a compliment. Unlike Israel (Jacob), Nathanael had no trace of cunning or deceit. He was transparent, without hypocrisy or craftiness. He wouldn't psychoanalyze your every sentence or look for hidden motives. His naivete' allowed people to impose on him. He probably would not have made a successful businessman. But his fortune, entered in heaven's computer, led him to the Pearl of great price.

This same Jesus who so angrily exposed the guile of the Pharisees and denounced their blatant hypocrisies, declared His evaluation of Nathanael's character as without sham or ulterior motives.

Nathanael was shocked. The questions he had formulated along the way to quiz Jesus vanished in the presence of this amazing Person. Bewildered and without guile, he asked, "How do You know me?" (see John 1:48)

Came the Messiah's doubt-crushing answer, "Before that Philip called thee, when thou wast under the fig tree, I saw thee" (v. 48). Somehow the omniscient Christ knew that Nathanael had been sitting under his fig tree in meditation before Philip arrived. Nathanael realized that Jesus knew his thoughts. Convinced, he exclaimed, "Rabbi, Thou art the Son of God; Thou art the King of Israel" (v. 49). This was a good confession, though perhaps not as deep as those of Peter and Thomas (Matt. 16:16; John 20:28).

Nathanael is an example of a sincere man who on evidence turned from bias to belief, and from skepticism to conviction. My library contains a book, *The Conversion of St. Paul* by Lord Lyttleton, who was an 18th century member of Parliament and of British nobility. The preface tells how it and another book entitled *Observations on the Resurrection of Christ* came to be written. Lyttleton and a friend, Gilbert West, were fully persuaded that the Bible was untrue, and determined to expose it as such. To destroy Christianity, they decided to disprove certain well-known Bible stories. Lyttleton chose the conversion of Paul, while West tackled the Resurrection of Christ. Taking ample time, they sat down to their respective tasks full of prejudice. Later when they compared notes, they discovered that each had become convinced from his private study that the Bible records were true. The results of their research were the two scholarly works just mentioned, both in defense of Christianity.

## Nathanael Found Fuller Knowledge

Some would classify Nathanael as the mystic, otherworldly, absent-minded-professor-type among the Twelve. True or not, Jesus did promise him, " 'Because I said unto thee, "I saw thee under the fig tree," believest thou? Thou shalt see greater things than these.' And He saith unto him, 'Verily, verily, I say unto you, hereafter ye shall see heaven open, and the angels of God ascending and descending upon the Son of man' " (John 1:50-51).

What was Jesus referring to? Several explanations have been given, such as Jesus' Ascension into heaven or the glorious Second Coming from heaven. But neither of these seems quite right. Instead Jesus was referring to Jacob's ladder vision during his flight from home. On this ladder which reached from earth to heaven, angels were ascending and descending (Gen. 28:12). The reflective Nathanael would come to see how Jesus Christ was the fulfillment of that ladder by linking earth and heaven through His redemptive work. Perhaps Nathanael had been reading that very story of Jacob's ladder when Philip told him about Jesus.

Along with the others Nathanael saw Jesus perform miracles, speak graciously, and forgive sinners. Wonder followed wonder: the deaf heard, the blind saw, the mute spoke, the lepers were cleansed, the crowds fed, the storm stilled, and the dead raised. Though sometimes puzzled, Nathanael knew he was living, walking, and eating in the very presence of the Son of God.

Then came the night of betrayal, arrest, and scourging, followed by the Crucifixion. From then till the Resurrection, Nathanael's faith, along with that of the others, seemed to die. Then Jesus rose, forcing the miracle of the Resurrection inescapably upon their hearts, and prompting a renewal of life that motivated them to carry the message of divine forgiveness to the ends of the earth.

Somewhere along the line it had dawned on Nathanael that Jesus was the Ladder that spanned the barrier between heaven and earth, making it possible for sinful man to be reconciled to a holy God.

Man has made many attempts to reach heaven. Like the builders of the Tower of Babel, man has brought his bricks of good deeds to build skyward. But such attempts only result in failure. Nathanael came to see that God was setting up a ladder in the person of His Son. Christ, who was without sin, took our sin on Him. He spanned the gulf so that God could reach out and accept unrighteous man through His righteousness.

Nathanael's vision is still vital today. Christ is the Way, the Bread, the Water, the Life, and the *Ladder*. How foolish for us to try to reach God on our own when a ladder has already been provided. A religious citizen dreamed he was building a ladder to heaven. When he did a good deed, the ladder went up one more step. When he gave a dollar to charity, he added another step. When he joined the church, the ladder went up 10 steps. Higher and higher went the ladder till it reached beyond the clouds and out of sight. As the end of his life neared, the man thought that surely the ladder would extend clear up into heaven by then. So confidently stepping off the top of the ladder, thinking it heaven, he found nothing there and went tumbling head over heels to his ruin. As he passed all the starry host, he heard a clap of thunder from which came a voice, "He that climbeth up some other way, the same is a thief and a robber" (John 10:1). Awaking from his dream, he recalled the verse which says that Jesus is the Way, apart from whom no man can reach the Father (14:6).

Jesus Christ was Nathanael's ladder. And yours too, if you trust Him.

# Thomas, the Questioner

When I was in my freshman year of high school, my English teacher called on me to answer a question. But she got my last name mixed up with the boy across from me, whose name was Lee. Hesitating, she called out the first two letters of Flynn, then added his name, Lee. The result was FLEE. But she pointed at me. Because I was small, the class thought she meant FLEA. That nickname stuck all the way through high school.

Because of Thomas' nickname of "doubter," we tend to think of him as a villainous character. Indeed he did want proof of Christ's resurrection, demanding to examine the nailprints before he would believe. He has been dubbed "The Palestinian who came from Missouri." But does this incident justify the label he has carried through the centuries?

Unquestionably his nickname contains an element of truth, but also borders on the misleading. If doubt was his outstanding characteristic, it was honest doubt. He had a questioning mind that desired to know the truth. Once convinced of the answer, he followed the truth wholeheartedly.

Jesus gave no hint that He was offended by Thomas' doubt. Thomas' exclamation of belief in the final, mind-boggling miracle of the Resurrection stands climactic among the several proofs of Christ's deity in the Gospel of John. His sincere doubt has helped multitudes to arrive at intelligent belief. Instead of "doubting" Thomas, a better description would be "questioning" Thomas.

Thomas is not mentioned in the first three Gospels, except in the listings of the Twelve: seventh in Matthew (10:3), eighth both in Mark (3:18) and in Luke (6:15). He is listed sixth among the disciples in the Upper Room after the Resurrection (Acts 1:13). In the Book of John, Thomas comes alive through three separate episodes. John also gives us his other name—Didymus (11:16)—and includes him among the seven disciples who went fishing after the Resurrection, which may suggest his occupation (21:2).

Thomas did seem to have a melancholy side to his nature. Some suggest he was in poor health. Yet despite his inadequacies, he was a man of loyalty and courage. Though pessimistic, he was devoted, ready to die for Christ. Perhaps his twofold nature makes his other name, Didymus or "twin," so appropriate. On the one hand, he was gloomy; but on the other hand, he was heroic.

The symbol for Thomas is a carpenter's square and a spear, because tradition says he erected a church with his own hands in the subcontinent of India to which he became a missionary and where he died a martyr, kneeling in prayer.

He was a man divided—a doubter, then a believer. Let's look at the three incidents involving Thomas.

### His Brave Pessimism (John 11:1-16)

Our first glimpse of Thomas in action comes toward the close of Jesus' ministry, just before the raising of Lazarus from the dead. Though the Master was immensely popular, the religious leaders intensely hated Him. More than once they tried to incite the mobs to stone Him to death. Leaving the danger zone of Jerusalem, Jesus led His disciples to the comparative safety of Perea, across the Jordan from Judea.

Suddenly word reached them that Jesus' beloved friend, Lazarus, was seriously ill. After a two-day wait Jesus announced His intent to journey back to Bethany to see Lazarus. But the disciples were frightened. "Don't You remember how they tried to stone You recently? And You're going back there again?" (see v. 8)

Despite the opposition, Jesus reaffirmed His purpose: "Our friend Lazarus sleepeth; but I go, that I may awake him out of sleep" (v. 11). Replied the disciples, "If he sleep, he shall do well" (v. 12). As usual, the disciples misunderstood. They thought Jesus was referring to physical rest, not death.

Then Jesus told them plainly that Lazarus was dead, adding that their faith would benefit from what He would do (vv. 14-15). He had earlier promised that this sickness would be for the glory of God (v. 4).

How did the disciples react to Jesus' desire to return to Judea? For a moment, no one said anything. But while they looked away in the distance, or shuffled their sandals, or cleared their throats, Thomas spoke up, "Let us also go, that we may die with Him" (v. 16). He affirmed his readiness to follow his Master back to Bethany, even if it meant death.

Doesn't his courage tell us something which more than offsets his supposed skepticism? As the Twelve headed back to the land of danger in what seemed a reckless act of suicide, Peter may have been at the head of the group. But it was Thomas who sparked the courage that rallied their faltering loyalty. Thomas did die for Christ, but not for some years.

However, Thomas' courage was tinged with morbidity. Ahead he could see only disaster. Though he was devoted, his voice reflected gloom and disaster. He was a constituted pessimist who could see only the dark side of things. His concept of Jesus was limited. He didn't sense that Jesus could and would raise Lazarus from the dead. Even though he was courageous, death loomed large in Thomas' vision.

But let's not be too hard on him. Didn't Martin Luther have fits of depression, even throwing an inkwell at the devil? Bunyan wrote of Doubting Castle and Giant Despair. From the depths of despair the Prophet Elijah prayed, "It is enough; now, O Lord, take away my life" (1 Kings 19:4). Even David cried out, expressing our frequent mood, "Why art thou cast down, O my soul?" (Ps. 42:5)

**His Heavy-Hearted Bewilderment** (John 14:1-7)
The second incident revealing Thomas' character took place in the Upper Room the eve of Christ's crucifixion. Jesus had just observed the Passover, and was giving His farewell address. The disciples were devastated. Their cherished hopes and dreams of recent months were quickly dissipating. They were sure that their earlier fears of danger in Jerusalem were about to come true. This was to be finis for Jesus and for their association with Him.

But Jesus was trying to make them understand it was not the end, but really the beginning. "I go to prepare a place for you. And if I go and prepare a place for you, I will come again and receive you unto Myself; that where I am, there ye may be also" (vv. 2-3). He was trying to get them to see that blessings lay beyond the Cross.

Then He added a statement that puzzled Thomas. "And whither I go ye know, and the way ye know" (v. 4). Unable to contain himself, Thomas blurted out, "Lord, we know not whither Thou goest; and how can we know the way?" (v. 5) Thomas' blind spot was his inability to comprehend that Jesus' mission reached beyond the boundaries of death. He wondered how Jesus could establish an earthly kingdom if He retired to heaven. Perhaps his question stemmed more from confusion than from unbelief. Thomas' query contained a certain amount of honest doubt.

Thomas represents those people who must have reasons for everything. However, the Christian faith does not let us see life all worked out in advance, but requires that we walk by faith. To know Christ is sufficient.

Whatever tones of understanding and gloom Thomas' question may have demonstrated, we shall be forever indebted to him because of the answer Jesus gave. Jesus replied, "I am the way, the truth and the life; no man cometh unto the Father but by Me" (v. 6).

To reach God and heaven we must go through Christ. He is the model, the teacher, the giver of eternal life. Christ is the answer exclusively. He is the fulfillment of Old Testament prophecies, types and symbols, the sole Mediator between God and man. To those who trust Him, He becomes the Alpha and Omega, the all-in-all.

**His Honest Skepticism** (John 20:24-28)

The third occasion Thomas receives mention in John's Gospel concerns the Resurrection. His gloom reached its lowest ebb with the cross and tomb. Somehow he was not present the first night when Jesus appeared to the disciples in the Upper Room. Perhaps he was roaming the rocky ravines or climbing the lonely hills, shedding tears in solitary sadness.

Why was he missing? If anything like modern Thomases who miss meetings with fellow-believers, he may have given the excuse, "I've worked hard all day. I'm tired. That mile walk to the Upper Room will make me sleepy."

Someone wrote a true confession titled, "Lord, I Lied!" It went like this. "Almighty God, as I sit here tonight, surrounded by newspapers and half watching television, it has just come to me that I have lied to Thee and to myself. I said I was too tired to go to church tonight. That was not true. I would have gone to a baseball game, or any other place I had wanted to go. Being too tired seemed to cover up my indifference. God, have mercy on me; I have lied to Thee and to myself. I am not too tired, I am indifferent. Warm my cold heart, O God, for that is the real reason why I stayed home. Amen."

The real reason Thomas missed that meeting was because he didn't expect Jesus to be there. He didn't believe Christ had risen from the dead. He told the others, in effect, "You go and mourn together if you like, but He won't be present."

The Christian mayor of a large Canadian city told his secretary immediately after his election, "No appointments are to be made for me under any circumstances on Wednesday nights." When his secretary looked at him questioningly, the mayor explained, "I have an appointment with my Lord every Wednesday night, and I try not to fail to go meet Him. I will make no other appointments." While serving as mayor of that city, he maintained his practice of regular attendance at midweek prayer service.

We deprive ourselves of numerous benefits when we don't worship at the Lord's house. Thomas missed several.

*He missed the presence of Christ.* When rumors of the empty tomb began to circulate, the disciples met together in the Upper Room. Behind shut doors they discussed the bewildering events of the day. Suddenly, without opening a door, Jesus came and stood in their midst. But Thomas was absent.

When F. D. Roosevelt was President, the phone rang in the office of a Washington church. "Will the President be in his church Sunday morning?" a voice asked. The minister replied, "That I cannot promise. But I do know the Lord will be present, and that should be sufficient incentive for a reasonably large attendance."

The Lord Jesus has promised to be present where two or three are gathered in His name (Matt. 18:20).

*He missed the teaching of the Word of God.* That night the Lord opened the understanding of those present by showing how the Law of Moses, the Prophets, and the poetical books all predicted His sufferings and Resurrection. Doubtless, like the Emmaus disciples who received similar instruction, the disciples' hearts burned within them as their minds were illumined. But Thomas missed this magnificent course in Old Testament prophecy.

*He missed the fellowship of believers.* Like the other 10, Thomas still had rough spots which needed divine polishing. But he missed out on the mutual edification that comes through the communion of believers.

Admittedly, no church is composed of perfect people. However, for the most part believers are God's choice gems. He has established His church for our maturity. From the mutuality of common worship and service, God's people derive strength and growth.

*He missed joy and peace.* The disciples went to this meeting gloomy. Reports were floating around that their Master was alive. But they met together, except for Peter to whom Jesus had earlier appeared, to lament a dead Christ. Then, behold, He stood in their midst. No wonder the disciples were glad when they saw the living Lord.

Then Jesus pronounced a benediction on the disciples, "Peace be unto you" (John 20:19). Thomas missed both peace and joy.

How often people, down in the dumps, walk into a church and there receive instruction and inspiration that helps them find, maintain, or renew a right relationship with Christ.

*He missed the commission of Christ.* At this meeting the Lord told them that "repentance and remission of sins should be preached in His name among all nations, beginning at Jerusalem." He commissioned them as witnesses, "As My Father hath sent Me, even so send I you" (Luke 24:47-48; John 20:21). He gave them a job to do, but Thomas didn't receive his assignment then.

*He missed seeing the wounds of Christ.* To dispel the disciples' fright at what they supposed was a ghost, Jesus showed them His hands, feet, and side. Then He invited them to touch Him to be sure. The nail prints made such an impression on them that in reporting Christ's appearance to Thomas they mentioned His wounds. Because of this emphasis Thomas gave his famous reply of skepticism, "Except I shall see in His hands the print of the nails, and put my finger into the print of the nails, and thrust my hand into His side, I will not believe" (John 20:25).

Thomas refused to believe the testimony of Mary Magdalene, the women, the Emmaus disciples or the other 10 apostles. He demanded a pragmatic test. "I must see and feel for myself."

One Greek word for *doubt* means literally "to judge between" or to choose between two views. A tribe on the eastern slope of the lofty Peruvian Andes describes doubt accurately by the simple phrase, "to have two thoughts." Doubt implies wavering between this and that. A person who holds one view but is willing to examine another with an open mind has an excellent chance of learning the truth. Honest doubt can be transformed into strong conviction. This happened to Thomas.

Though despairingly doubtful, Thomas was willing to be convinced. The other apostles' unanimous and repeated affirmations of seeing Christ back from the dead convinced Thomas to attend their meeting the next Sunday in the Upper Room. And he was not disappointed. Jesus came, "the doors being shut, and stood in the midst, and said, 'Peace be unto you.' " His eyes began to search for Thomas. "Reach hither thy finger, and behold My hands; and reach hither thy hand, and thrust it unto My side: and be not faithless, but believing" (vv. 26-27).

Thomas had been looking for evidence. Here it was: indisputable, tangible, overwhelming. How often he had seen those hands as they touched fevered brows, gave instant sight to blind eyes, or blessed little children. It was His Master. There was no need to put his finger into the nail prints. Almost before Jesus finished speaking, Thomas exclaimed, perhaps on his knees, "My Lord and my God" (v. 28). This confession acknowledged Jesus as God, surpassing all other affirmations uttered previously by any and all disciples. Thomas' sullen skepticism turned to shining faith.

Jesus blames no one for wanting evidence. Which is better: a faith which accepts blindly, or a faith which seeks proof? Jesus knew that once Thomas, or any other doubter, had fought his way through doubt, he would end up the surest man in the neighborhood. Much harm can be caused by religious gullibility. The Christian faith is not intellectually disrespectable, but rests on a reasonable basis. Thus every believer is required to be able to give a defense for his belief. An honest doubter can become a strong believer. Thomas doubted that we might be sure.

Because of Thomas' experience we learn of another available blessing. Jesus said, "Thomas, because thou hast seen Me, thou hast believed: blessed are they that have not seen, and yet have believed" (v. 29). Only a few hundred saw the risen Christ. Untold thousands have never seen Him except through the eye of faith. For Thomas and his contemporaries, seeing was believing. For us, believing is seeing.

Jesus seemed to be saying something like this, "Thomas, many skeptics will want to see the same as you have seen. I would like to do the same for them, as I have done for you, and show them My wounds. But that's impossible. Yet they will be able to see Me. They will see Me through your eyes, and the eyes of the apostles and others to whom I appeared. They will come to believe through your witness. Thus, they will believe without seeing because they accept your testimony. They too will come to confess Me as Lord and God. For them, believing will be seeing. And that's more blessed than believing through seeing."

Thomas could never forget Christ's scars. They had been marks of recognition. They were reminders of the agonizing sufferings of his Saviour. And they continued to be marks of ownership, ever recalling the truth that he had been purchased, not "with corruptible things, as silver and gold . . . but with the precious blood of Christ" (1 Peter 1:18-19). He no longer could say what he wished, look at what he wanted, do what he desired, or walk where he willed. Owned by Christ, his tongue, eyes, hands, and feet—his entire body and intellect—belonged to Him. Those wounds were constant reminders of the Master's ownership.

A small orphaned boy lived with his grandmother. One night their house caught on fire. The grandmother, trying to rescue the little boy asleep upstairs, perished in the flames. A crowd gathered around the burning house. The boy's cries for help were heard above the crackling of the blaze. No one seemed to know what to do, for the front of the house was a mass of flames. Suddenly a stranger rushed from the crowd and circled to the back where he spotted an iron pipe that reached an upstairs window. He disappeared for a minute, then reappeared with the boy in his arms. Mid the cheers of the crowd, he climbed down the hot pipe as the boy hung around his neck.

Weeks later a public meeting was held in the town hall to determine in whose custody the boy would be placed. Each person wanting the boy was permitted to speak briefly. The first man said, "I have a big farm. Everybody needs the out-of-doors." The second man told the advantages he could provide. "I'm a teacher. I have a large library. He would get a good education." Others spoke. Finally the richest man in the community said, "I'm wealthy. I could give the boy everything mentioned tonight: farm, books, education, and more, including money and travel. I would like to have him live in my home."

The chairman asked, "Anyone else like to say a word?" From

the back seat rose a stranger who had slipped in unnoticed. As he walked toward the front, deep suffering showed on his face. Reaching the front of the room, he stood directly in front of the little boy. Slowly the stranger removed his hands from his pockets. A gasp went up from the crowd. The little boy, whose eyes had been focused on the floor till now, looked up. The man's hands were terribly scarred. Suddenly the boy emitted a cry of recognition. Here was the man who had saved his life. His hands were scarred from climbing up and down the hot pipe. With a leap the boy threw himself around the stranger's neck and held on for life.

The farmer rose and left. The teacher, too. Then the rich man. Everyone departed, leaving the boy and his rescuer who had won him without a word. Those marred hands spoke more effectively than any words.

Today many interests vie for our devotion. Young and old alike are challenged by the call of money, education, fame, pleasure, and a host of other voices. But let us never forget that down the corridors of the centuries walks One who, by merely raising His hands, reminds us of His claim upon us. Those nail-pierced hands say,

> I gave My life for thee
> My precious blood I shed,
> That thou might'st ransomed be,
> And quickened from the dead;
> I gave, I gave My life for thee,
> What hast thou giv'n for Me?

Through the ages, Thomas has had many twins who, like him, have doubted the Christian faith. If you are such a doubter, may honest investigation into the claims of Jesus Christ lead you to say with Thomas, "My Lord and my God."

# 9

# Matthew, the Tax Collecter

While attending seminary a young man managed an apartment complex. He and his wife established close friendships with their tenants by inviting them to their apartment for refreshments, going out to eat with them, and relaxing with them around the swimming pool. They hoped for an opportunity to present the Gospel.

Once a month, a Christian couple invited different unsaved friends and neighbors to their house for dinner, then showed a Moody science film. Usually the ensuing conversation turned easily to the subject of God and led to an unforced presentation of the Gospel.

These incidents represent a method of witness known as "dinner evangelism." But dinner evangelism is not a 20th-century innovation. Matthew, one of the Twelve, engaged in this type of witness immediately after his conversion.

Several disciples were double-named, among them Matthew. In the first Gospel he is called *Matthew* (Matt. 9:9; 10:3). But in Mark and Luke he is called, first *Levi,* who sat at the receipt of custom, then later listed as *Matthew* (Mark 2:14; 3:18; Luke 5:27; 6:15). Possibly his earlier name was *Levi,* and his post-conversion name, *Matthew*, given him by Jesus who had also given other disciples new names. Or Levi may just refer to the tribe from which he came. In Mark and Luke he is listed seventh in the apostolic band, and in Matthew and Acts he ranks eighth (Acts 1:13).

Mark calls Matthew the son of Alphaeus (Mark 2:14). James the Less is also called the son of Alphaeus (Matt. 10:3). Some assume, without proof, that Matthew and James the Less were brothers. If so, there were at least three sets of brothers among the disciples.

We know very little about Matthew. But even though our information on him is minimal, we can tell much about him by his occupation.

## Matthew's Despised Occupation

In his own Gospel, Matthew calls himself a publican (10:3). But the other Gospel writers graciously neglect to mention his contemptible profession. By mentioning his type of work Matthew was confessing, "I couldn't have been engaged in a more despicable business. No more unlikely candidate for apostleship ever lived." His social status would be equivalent to that of modern-day Mafia members or dope-sellers. He had a right to his sense of unworthiness.

Fiercely disliked by the general public, publicans were divided by the Talmud into two classes. One group, the *gabbai* or general tax collectors, collected taxes on wine, fruit, and similar items. Matthew belonged to the second group, the *mikhsa* or custom-house officials. These tax collectors were despised because they could stop people, search them, or pierce their baggage with long, sharp iron rods, looking for contraband.

With his office just outside Capernaum, Matthew had an ideal location. The heavily loaded caravans moving down the main highway from Damascus to Jerusalem had to stop at his customs-house and pay import taxes, ranging anywhere from 2 to 12 percent. Matthew also received a tax from fishermen on the nearby Sea of Galilee. Perhaps Peter, Andrew, James, and John had often paid him tax.

Hour after hour the coins rattled into Matthew's register. Day by day he sensed deep hatred in the eyes of those who did business in his office. Naturally, no one liked to have customs officials run their hands through his luggage. But there were more reasons why tax collectors were hated.

First, most publicans were dishonest. After paying a fixed amount to Rome to buy the job, they could then pocket all in excess, thus tempting them to make as big a personal rake-off from the people as possible. Greed, graft, fraud, extortion, and corruption followed in the wake. With the power of the Roman Empire behind them, enforced by the presence of Roman soldiers, tax collectors could cajole and threaten the people into paying exorbitant fees. While the commoners suffered because of excessive taxes, the publicans were often wealthy.

Publicans were also hated because their employment in the service of Rome made them seem disloyal to their fellow Jews. Publicans were considered traitors and conspirators with a foreign government.

Thus, tax collecting was among the most odious of trades. Tax collectors were lumped together with heathen and harlots (Matt. 18:17; 21:31). A common epithet was "publicans and sinners" (9:10). Moreover, they were disqualified as witnesses in courts of law, scoffed at as common criminals, and refused admittance to the synagogue, where their money was also refused for alms. They were banished to the status of social lepers.

If Matthew was a typical publican, the love of money was a besetting sin. Attracted by the gleam of gold, he sold his conscience and turned renegade to his native land. His occupation was lucrative. The more he cheated, the richer he grew. But he lost his religious privileges and became an outcast. Perhaps when starting out he had intended to be honest, but he gradually fell into the traps of his detestable trade. His heart became hardened to the cry of the widowed and orphaned.

## Matthew's Gracious Call

Since Capernaum became Jesus' headquarters after He left Nazareth, Matthew must have heard of Jesus again and again. This miracle-worker became the talk of the town. In Capernaum Jesus healed Peter's mother-in-law. As a result, all the city gathered at Peter's door to bring their sick for Jesus to heal. Matthew, the rich tax collector certainly knew what was going on.

Then one day Matthew heard how Simon, along with his brother and cousins, had given up their business to follow Jesus. Later he heard how Jesus had healed the palsied man whom friends let down through the roof. Moreover, Jesus had said to the paralytic, "Thy sins are forgiven thee" (Mark 2:3-5). In his inner being, Matthew probably wished his sins could be forgiven.

One day, wondering if Jesus would accept a despised publican, Matthew suddenly sensed someone standing in his booth. Looking up from his accounts, he gazed straight into the face of Jesus. Under the scrutiny of Jesus, Matthew began to feel his own vileness as never before. He felt so dirty on the inside. Would Jesus call him names as other people did, "Publican, sinner, traitor, swindler"?

Jesus graciously said, "Follow Me" (Matt. 9:9). Overwhelmed at the invitation, overjoyed at the welcome, Matthew immediately felt pure. His conscience no longer tormented him. He was full of peace. He recalled the words of Jesus to His critics after healing the palsied man and absolving him of his sins, "The Son of man hath power on earth to forgive sins" (v. 6). Incidentally, Matthew places this statement directly prior to his call to follow Jesus (v. 9).

He obeyed immediately, closing his ledgers, putting down his quill, stumbling out from behind his desk, and shutting his booth. Luke wrote, "And after these things He went forth, and saw a publican, named Levi, sitting at the receipt of custom: and He said unto him, 'Follow Me.' And he left all, rose up, and followed Him" (Luke 5:27-28). Other professing followers would ask to bury their dead, say good-bye to their families, or handle some other situation before following Jesus—but Matthew's response was immediate.

The poet puts it,

> I heard His call, "Come follow,"
> That was all.

My gold grew dim,
My soul went after Him,
I rose and followed.
That was all.
Who would not follow
If they heard Him call?

Matthew experienced the matchless, marvelous, wonderful grace of Jesus. No matter how dark his deeds nor how deep the strain, he received 100 percent forgiveness. He was gloriously lifted to honorable apostleship. How meaningful his name, Matthew, "gift of God." What hope this act of Jesus gives to all who have stumbled along life's path. Undeserved favor is available for all.

Jesus' choice of Matthew would seem poor public relations. In the first place, Matthew's presence would radically alter the composition of the apostles up to that time. Since Matthew is listed seventh on two lists, it's likely six of the apostles were called before him: Andrew, Peter, James, John, Philip, and Nathanael. These men were fishermen and patriots. To have the disliked, traitorous tax collector of Capernaum thrust into their midst would introduce tension among this intimate band.

Secondly, such a policy would alienate the general public. For Jesus to call a moral leper seemed politically imprudent. All would be shocked, especially the holier-than-thou religious leaders who complained, "This man eateth with publicans and sinners" (see Luke 15:2). Wouldn't the presence of Matthew among the inner group be a stumbling block to Jewish prejudice and turn off the crowds? To the orthodox Jews, Jesus' choice was unthinkable.

But Jesus' selection demonstrated the availability of forgiveness for the worst of people. Not just nice people are candidates for divine pardon. God's love knows no bounds; His grace reaches to all. Whereas others looked on Matthew with hate, Jesus saw a man who needed the gift of love. This same gift is free to all who have sinned and repent.

Also, the introduction of an alien figure into the apostleship was part of His strategy for reaching all classes of people. If all types were to be included in the church, then it would take more than fishermen to evangelize the world. Diversity would have to be found among the evangels.

Interestingly, Moody's famous song leader, Ira Sankey, was engaged in the tax collecting business, though honestly. Converted at 16, Sankey met Moody at an 1870 YMCA convention at Indianapolis. Moody at once recognized in Sankey God's fulfillment of his longtime search for a Gospel singer. "Where have you been? I've waited 18 years for you," exclaimed Moody. He insisted that Sankey give up his position in Pennsylvania and join him in his campaigns across the United States and Europe.

But 30-year-old Sankey, with parents, a wife, and three sons, at first resisted Moody's recruiting efforts. He had established himself in his home-state as chief tax officer in a revenue bureau. Son of a bank president, he enjoyed a comfortable lifestyle and anticipated a career in federal service with all its rewards and pleasures.

But Moody was convinced that God's will was otherwise. Finally Sankey agreed to join the dynamic evangelist on a trial basis. In mid-1871, Sankey traveled to Chicago to team up in a series of meetings, beginning an association which lasted nearly 30 years. What a loss it would have been had Sankey chosen to retain his tax collector's job. But like Matthew before him, he followed God's path.

## Matthew's Generous Feast

Immediately after accepting Jesus' call, "Levi made Him a great feast in his own house: and there was a great company of publicans and of others that sat down with them" (Luke 5:29). The facts of the feast, the long list of invited guests, and a house and property spacious enough to handle the crowd, all point to Matthew's wealth. But for Matthew, it was money well spent, for the dinner served several purposes.

*Celebration.* Matthew was so happy for his new life. The misery of the past was gone. This has been called Matthew's spiritual wedding feast, commemorating the marriage of his soul to the Saviour. The feast came from a grateful heart.

So many references to dinners occur in the Bible: the Parable of the Wedding Feast, the meal at Mary and Martha's, the meal with the Emmaus disciples, the feeding of the 5,000 and 4,000, and the Lord's Supper, for example.

Just as emancipation from Egyptian bondage brought forth the song of Moses and the Lamb, so Matthew's freedom from his guilt and slavery brought praise from his heart. The dinner expressed his delight. Jesus, to whom he owed it all, was his guest of honor.

*Good-bye.* Matthew was burning his bridges behind him. He was saying to his fellow-workers that he was quitting his trade. He was giving public notice of his new identification with the kingdom of Christ. It was a sort of going-away party, the semi-equivalent of baptism in which he was confessing his death to the old life, and his rebirth to a new career.

*Witness.* Matthew wanted to witness to his old cronies, so he invited them to dinner. If he invited pious people, they would have avoided him, for only publicans and sinners would set foot in his house. Would Jesus be there? Even if every sinner in Galilee and Judea were coming, Jesus would accept the invitation. He was known as the friend of sinners.

What a sight it must have been! Matthew was at the head of the table, and Jesus in the seat of honor. Then all around, according to one version, "a multitude" of social outcasts, the scum of society though indeed well-dressed, greedy, money-hungry men, sat astonished at the step their fellow tax collector had taken. If any of them had the slightest desire for a better life, Matthew knew they could find it in Jesus. So he presented Him to all his guests.

Just as Andrew brought Peter, and Philip evangelized Nathanael, so Matthew wanted to introduce his friends to Jesus. He used the imaginative strategy of a meal.

The religious leaders heard about this dinner. Ever on the lookout for scandal, they murmured against both Jesus and His disciples for eating with sinners. Jesus, who had not condemned any of the outcasts present, rebuked the religious people, "They that are whole need not a physician; but they that are sick. I came not to call the righteous, but sinners to repentance (Luke 5:30-32).

Jesus reserved His harshest words for the self-righteous religious people who thought they had no need of mercy. During the final week of His ministry, Jesus said to the Pharisees, "The publicans and the harlots go into the kingdom of God before you" (Matt. 21:31). Once in response to the repeated grumblings of the Pharisees that He received and ate with sinners, Jesus gave three beautiful parables, one after another: the lost sheep, the lost coin, and the lost son. He showed that just as joy greeted the finding of these three lost items, so heaven rejoices when one lost sinner repents. The Pharisees, by sulking like the elder brother, placed themselves out of tune with the Father's heart (Luke 15).

Sam Shoemaker, an Episcopalian leader, once wrote that the best position for a Christian to take was just inside the door of salvation. If one gets too far inside, he tends to forget what it's like on the outside. If he's too far removed from the door, he cannot help blind, groping seekers find the entrance.

A church in a Chilean city held nightly meetings with a wide welcome to all neighborhood citizens. As thieves sneaked out night after night on their crooked errands, they would hear the joyful singing, listen for a while, and go on their rounds. But some thieves slipped into the services, were convicted of their sins, and repented. A year later the police did something almost unprecedented in evangelistic annals. They sent the pastor a New Year's card containing the photographs of 24 criminals. They suggested that these photos should be filed in the church records since the men had left their thieving careers as a result of hearing the pastor's Gospel messages.

## Matthew's Literary Ability

The average person in Matthew's day would have thought this tax collector couldn't change. But Jesus saw his potential. Matthew was keen, disciplined, good with figures, and acquainted with Aramaic, Greek, and Latin. Jesus, sensing Matthew was ready to give up money for meaning in life, transformed him and inspired him to write the first book of the New Testament.

Matthew's Gospel seems to be aimed at the Jews. He was determined to prove that Jesus was the true Messiah promised by the Old Testament prophets. This is why he so frequently used the formula, or something similar, in the two opening chapters, "This was done that it might be fulfilled which was spoken of the Lord by the prophet saying" (Matt. 1:22; 2:15, 17, 23).

The former bookkeeper was the ideal choice to trace the genealogy of Christ back through the royal line to David and Abraham, father of the Jews. Matthew's love of numbers shows up in the genealogy through his careful grouping of three sets of fourteen.

Matthew's fondness for systemization comes out in his topical arrangements. Though about half of his Gospel covers the same action as Mark, the characteristic feature of his Gospel is its great discourses. Chapters 5-7 contain the famous Sermon on the Mount. Chapter 10 gives the sermon on the proclamation of the kingdom uttered in connection with the sending out of the Twelve. Chapter 13 deals with the seven parables on the growth and worth of the kingdom. Chapter 18 handles lifestyle in the kingdom including humility, care for children's spiritual welfare, and forgiveness. Chapter 23 rocks with Christ's repeated woes on the hypocritical religious leaders who misled the people. Chapters 24 and 25 comprise the famous Olivet discourse dealing with the Second Coming. This man whose pen had been used in a despicable trade now served by taking down notes on Jesus' sermons. He dedicated his businesslike writing to the Lord.

Matthew was the forerunner of a great train of people who have been used in a writing ministry whether with figures or words: bookkeepers, treasurers, secretaries, editors, journalists, authors, poets.

Matthew spent the rest of his life sharing the glad news. Tradition says he evangelized in Ethiopia and Persia. His symbol—three purses—refers to his original occupation. Wherever he went he could testify of Christ's power to save to the uttermost. Perhaps he wrote Zacchaeus, chief publican of Jericho, urging him to see Jesus if ever He visited his city.

At Thanksgiving 1980, 250 "street people" in New York City were handed formal, engraved invitations which read: "The honor of your presence is required at a banquet at the Lamb's given in your honor because of Jesus and His love." The banquet was sponsored by members of the Manhattan Church of the Nazarene. The church was called "Lamb's" because of its location in a former New York nightclub by that name.

Around 200 people came, some who daily scrounged for scraps of food in garbage cans. They sat at tables covered with tablecloths, fine china, and silverware. Tuxedoed maitre d's escorted guests to their seats. Waiters in white shirts and ties served a traditional Thanksgiving meal. Guests were also treated to a concert by a local Gospel music group before dinner.

Fifty members of the church helped prepare and serve the meal. Five Iowa farmers brought in $1,000 worth of goods by trucks and stayed to help with the cooking. Six women from an upstate prayer group baked 42 pies. At the end the pastor gave a brief talk, explaining how to be born again. Twenty-five people went forward to indicate their decision to receive Christ. Because of the banquet, more people began to attend the church.

Matthew's dinner strategy keeps going on.

# 10

# James, the Less and Judas, not Iscariot: Forgotten Followers

A legend tells how, as construction started on a new cathedral, the angel in charge promised a rare prize to the person who made the most important contribution to the finished sanctuary. As the building went up, people speculated as to who would win the prize. The architect? The contractor? The woodcutter? The artisans skilled in gold, iron, brass, and glass? Perhaps the carpenter assigned the detailed grill work near the altar? Because each workman did his best, the completed church was a masterpiece. But when the moment came to announce the contest winner, what a surprise when the prize was awarded to an old, poorly dressed peasant woman. What had she done? Every day she had faithfully carried hay to the ox that pulled the marble for the stonecutter.

Little things and inconspicuous people are important. Strangely, we have very little information on most of the apostles. This is especially true of the two subjects of this chapter. Judas, known also as Lebbaeus and Thaddaeus, asked one question of Jesus in the Upper Room. Of James the Less no record exists of anything he said or did. Nevertheless these two men were chosen by Jesus to be members of the Twelve, and played a significant part in fulfilling their Master's Great Commission. They are typical of the thousands of forgotten followers of Christ, unsung heroes who through the centuries have consistently but quietly done His work.

## Judas—Lebbaeus—Thaddaeus

Two of the Twelve were called Judas, a popular name in those days. Note that when John wrote that this Judas asked Jesus a question in the Upper Room, he carefully distinguished him from the traitor, specifying "Judas . . . , not Iscariot" (John 14:22). He wished to spare him the shame of identification with the infamous Judas.

Perhaps the stigma attached to that name caused Matthew and Mark to use Judas' other names. Matthew called him "Lebbaeus, whose surname was Thaddaeus" (Matt. 10:3) Mark called him "Thaddaeus" (Mark 3:18). But Luke called him "Judas" (Luke 6:16; Acts 1:13). Comparison of lists shows these three names referred to the same person. Church-father Jerome called him "Trinomius," which means "the man with three names." Both Lebbaeus and Thaddaeus carry the idea "beloved" or "warmhearted" or "full of heart," thus courageous.

Little is known of his family. Though the King James version calls him Judas "the brother of James" (Luke 6:16), later versions change this phrase to "the son of James." The original contains neither "brother" nor "son," simply "Judas of James." When names are thus connected, it usually means the first person is a son of the second.

Some erroneously believe Judas to be a brother of James, and also hold that James was the brother of Jesus, thus making Judas a brother of Jesus too. Jesus *did* have a brother by the name of Judas (Matt. 13:55). But the Apostle Judas could not have been Jesus' brother, because none of His brothers believed on Him till after the Resurrection (John 7:5).

Another widely held misconception is that Judas of the Twelve wrote the Epistle of Jude. But that letter seems to have been written by the Judas who was a brother of James and Jesus (Jude 1). The author of Jude places himself out of the circle of the apostles when he speaks of them as "they" instead of "we" (Jude 17-18).

**Judas' Question** (John 14:22)
The only mention of anything Judas said or did is a question he asked Jesus in the Upper Room. Like the other disciples, he was perplexed. His hopes for an earthly kingdom were fast disappearing. A few days earlier when Jesus had ridden into Jerusalem on a colt with throngs hailing Him, and when He had cleansed the temple, things looked good. Perhaps Judas thought, *Finally He's going to reveal His true identity to everyone. And we'll be revealed with Him too.*

But Jesus didn't reveal Himself that way. After telling of the many mansions in His Father's house, and declaring Himself the way to the Father's home, He said, "I will not leave you comfortless: I will come to you. Yet a little while, and the world seeth Me no more; but ye see Me: because I live, ye shall live also. At that day ye shall know that I am in My Father, and ye in Me, and I in you. He that hath My commandments and keepeth them, he it is that loveth Me: and he that loveth Me shall be loved of My Father, and I will love him, and will manifest Myself to him (John 14:18-21).

It was then Judas asked, "Lord, how is it that Thou wilt manifest Thyself unto us, and not unto the world?" (v. 22) Perhaps Judas was indirectly suggesting, "Why not show Yourself in royal splendor, and claim the throne of our nation, then rule the world?"

Jesus' answer was really a rephrasing of what He had just said. "If a man love Me, he will keep My words: and My Father will love him, and We will come unto him, and make Our abode with him. He that loveth Me not keepeth not My sayings: and the word which ye hear is not Mine, but the Father's which sent Me" (vv. 23-24).

In effect, Jesus was saying, "Look, Judas, I cannot become the kind of King you want. That isn't the Father's will. My kingdom cannot be proclaimed sensationally nor spectacularly from the rooftops, nor through destruction of enemy armies. Rather, My kingdom of love will spread from one heart to another, and only this way will reach worldwide proportions.

"Some day I will manifest Myself openly as King of Kings. But the Cross must come before the crown. Tomorrow you'll see Me die. But you'll not be left alone. I'll be with you all the while you are keeping My word."

A pastor, visiting the bedside of an elderly shut-in, noticed an empty chair on the other side of the bed, placed at such an angle as to suggest that a visitor had just been there. When the pastor asked who the earlier visitor had been, the patient explained, "Years ago I found it impossible to pray. I fell asleep on my knees the minute I started because I was so tired. A friend told me I didn't have to kneel down, but just sit on the bed, pull up a chair opposite me, imagine Jesus in that chair, and talk to Him as I would to a friend. I've been doing it ever since."

A few days later the invalid died suddenly. His daughter lamented to the pastor, "I just left him for a few minutes, for he seemed to be sleeping so peacefully. When I returned, he had passed away. He hadn't moved since I saw him, except that his hand was reaching out toward the empty chair at the side of the bed. Do you understand?" Then the pastor explained the meaning of the empty chair.

Judas came to learn the meaning of Jesus' answer to his question. As he walked the paths of obedience, he knew Christ's comforting presence. Tradition says he preached in Edessa near the Euphrates River. Another account credits him with co-founding the church in Armenia, and then moving on to Kurdistan, where he was killed by arrows.

The symbol chosen for him is a ship, because of the many missionary journeys ascribed to him by tradition, and perhaps because he was thought to be a fisherman.

## James the Less

Three men with the name of James were close to Jesus. Too often the identify of these three has been confused in ecclesiastical art and history. For the record, the three were:

- James, one of the inner three of the Twelve, brother of John and one of the "sons of thunder," killed by Herod, the second recorded martyr in Acts.
- James, brother of Jesus, not found among Jesus' followers till

after the Resurrection, who became head of the Jerusalem church (Acts 1:14; 15:13; Gal. 2:9, 12).

• James the Less, ninth disciple in all lists (Matt. 10:3; Mark 3:18; Luke 6:15; Acts 1:13).

The New Testament tells us absolutely nothing of what James said or did, but does mention in all lists that he was the "son of Alphaeus." Mark tells us his mother was named Mary, though not the same Mary as Jesus' mother. Because of her devotion to Christ, she was among the women at the cross (Mark 15:40). Mark records that Mary was also the mother of Joses. Mark is the writer who gave James his nickname "the less" (v. 40).

To try to figure his exact relationships is exasperatingly futile. Since Alphaeus was the name of Matthew's father, some claim Matthew and James the Less were brothers, making another set of brothers among the Twelve (Mark 2:14). But this is pure conjecture. Because of similarity in the names of Alphaeus and Cleophas, some consider them to be the same person, thus making James the Less the son of Cleophas and Mary. But we are not told this.

Tradition doesn't have a lot to say about his missionary efforts, and there are conflicting accounts of how he died. One account says James the Less was stoned, but not fatally, then later sawed into pieces. The saw became his apostolic symbol.

James' nickname indicates inferiority. Literally "Less" means "little." The Greek word gives us our English *micro* as in microbe, microbiology, microcosm. Some think him younger in age, as compared with James the Elder, brother of John. One commentator even suggests he was the son of James, the brother of John, and thus a grandson of Zebedee.

Some suggest his inferiority was in his shortness of statute, translating his name "James the Little" or "Shorty" or "Little Jim."

Most think the "less" refers to rank or influence, as contrasted with James, the brother of John, one of the inner three. He would be "James Minor" as against "James Major." Others think his nickname was to distinguish him from James, brother of the Lord, who ultimately headed the Jerusalem church. James the Less has been called "James II."

## Importance of the Small

Many wonderful things in nature are petite. A common flea can jump 200 times its own height. A man with the same bounce could leap over Paris' Eiffel Tower. A fly can lift a match and move it along. A man with the same strength could carry a beam of lumber 24 feet long.

Tiny marks have their significance. A woman overseas cabled her husband, "Have found wonderful bracelet. Price $75,000. May I buy it?" The husband promptly wired back. "No, price too high." But the cable operator missed the signal for the comma. The woman received the message as, "No price too high." She bought the bracelet. The husband sued the telegraph company and won. No wonder users of Morse code now spell out punctuation.

Little omissions of duty can create havoc. "They won't miss me," said a mother as she repeatedly left her children to make the rounds of cocktail lounges. A fire broke out in her absence, taking the life of her two preschool children.

"They won't miss me," said the sentry as he left his post for a while. But during his absence the enemy surprised and wounded several of his comrades.

"They won't miss me," said a church member as he skipped a service one Sunday, then another Sunday, and then wondered why he no longer enjoyed an abundant Christian life.

On the other hand, little faithfulnesses lead to bigger tasks. Jesus said, "He that is faithful in that which is least is faithful also in much" (Luke 16:10). Little deeds of kindness repeated make it easier to do greater deeds of love. Courage to refuse temptation on a small occasion leads to courage in major situations.

Joseph's diligence in administering Potiphar's household fitted him for the assignment of ruling Egypt in days of famine. David, faithful in guarding the sheep out on the lonely hills against bears and lions, was readied for the larger task of shepherding Israel against the attacks of her enemies.

James the Less and Judas did their tasks unnoticed. Their aim was not fame, but faithfulness. Jesus, seeing potential in them, chose them to be among the Twelve, counting on them to make a significant contribution to the missionary cause. These two did their work faithfully, patiently, and humbly. Their gravestones could have recorded, "They have done what they could."

Down through the years God's work has been carried on mostly by little people doing little jobs, about whom little or nothing is known. The Lord's work could never be accomplished if it weren't for countless saints everywhere exercising their gifts. It has been pointed out that a lot can be accomplished in this world if we don't care who gets the credit. Many pastors labor sacrificially in out-of-the-way hamlets, whose voices are never heard on conference platforms nor on denominational boards. And many missionaries labor and die unhonored in remote corners of the earth.

A humble servant girl tried to join a church. "I've accepted Christ as my Saviour," she said to the deacon board. One official asked, "How do you know you have been converted?" She replied, "I'm quite sure because now I sweep under the rugs as well as around them." Christ's love had so filled her heart that she expressed it the best way she knew. She wasn't a great singer with a golden voice who could hold vast audiences spellbound. Nor could she paint brilliant pictures nor write literary masterpieces. But she could sweep under the rugs, remaining faithful in little things.

## Prevalence of the Unrecognized

The Bible has its unknown soldiers. The Nethinims were assigned the lower menial duties in the temple, but little is known of them (Ezra 2:43; 8:20). Who knows the name of the man who provided the colt on which Jesus rode into Jerusalem? And who was the man who furnished the Upper Room for the Last Supper? The names of the Wise Men are unknown. And who was the boy who gave his lunch to feed the 5,000?

Though we do know their names, so little is known of Judas and James the Less that they have been dubbed "patron saints of the unrecognized." They are representative of the numberless, nameless millions who have served the Lord faithfully through the centuries. They lead the army of forgotten followers.

Who preserved the Bible for us? Those men, known as Massoretes, wrote hour after hour and day after day, copying by hand with painstaking detail the sacred words of Scripture. When we see a great church, or a little one, we need to remember that probably a few forgotten people pooled their faith, vision, resources, and prayers to start that work years ago.

## Reward of the Faithful

Judas and James the Less had lowly spots in the lists of the Twelve. James was always ninth. Judas was twice 10th and twice 11th, really lowest rung on the ladder since 12th was reserved for Judas the traitor. But in the New Jerusalem, "the wall of the city had 12 foundations, and in them the names of the 12 apostles of the Lamb" (Rev. 21:14). Peter's name will not be carved any bigger than those of Judas and James the Less.

In that day we'll learn much about the lesser known of the Twelve, and about insignificant, passing names of the New Testament like Epaphroditus (Phil. 2:25), Stephanas (1 Cor. 16:15), Phoebe (Rom. 16:1-2), Nymphas (Col. 4:15), and Onesiphorus (2 Tim. 1:16). We'll find out more about the death of Antipas, "faithful martyr" (Rev. 2:13). We'll also meet a host of unnamed saints of all centuries who labored faithfully. Here on earth men may have their names inscribed on marble monuments for feats of fame. Some day those monuments will fall in fragments, but whoever does the will of God will abide forever.

Unknown servants will be honored for their insignificant but faithful service. "For God is not unrighteous to forget your work and labor of love, which ye have showed toward His name, in that ye have ministered to the saints, and do minister" (Heb. 6:10). Till then we should be steadfast, unmovable, always abounding in the work of the Lord.

Paul pointed out that some good works are noticed immediately. But "they that are otherwise" (slow to receive recognition) "cannot be hid," but must of necessity be ultimately recognized and rewarded in the day of reckoning (1 Tim. 5:25). Good deeds cannot be concealed forever.

When Mordecai reported a murderous plot and saved King

Ahasuerus' life, he received no credit. Mordecai may have thought with the passing of years that his deed would never be known. But one sleepless night, the king learned from reading the historical records that Mordecai had not only saved his life, but had gone unrewarded. The result was Mordecai's ultimate elevation to prime minister.

Many good deeds are performed without conscious fanfare or with deliberate anonymity. Those who blow their pious trumpets to attract attention receive their reward when people exclaim, "Isn't he a good man!" But those who don't will some day receive divine commendation and heavenly compensation.

One hot summer day back in the 1880's a young medical student was selling books house to house in a farming area of Maryland to earn money for college. Hot and thirsty near the end of the day, he called at a farmhouse where no one was home, except a cheerful teenage girl who said, "Mother's a widow. We have no money to buy books."

The student asked for a glass of cold water. She offered him a glass of cold milk instead. The thirsty student drank two glasses of milk. The girl would take no pay, explaining, "Mother told me to be kind to strangers."

Years later the medical student had become chief of surgery at a hospital. One day when visiting the wards, he spotted a face which he remembered as the one who had given him the glasses of cold milk long ago. The patient was very sick. The chief surgeon took a special interest in her case. She was moved into a private room with nurses round the clock. Everything known to medical science was done for her.

After weeks of care, the improving patient heard the nurse say, "You're going home tomorrow." At first the woman was delighted, then she murmured, "The cost of all this worries me—the bill must be very high." The nurse offered to get the bill.

Later, as the patient looked over the items and read the staggering cost of both the operation and her hospital care, tears filled her eyes. "How will I ever get it paid?" she exclaimed. But reading a little further down the page, she saw, "Paid in full by a glass of milk. Howard A. Kelly, M.D."

# 11

# Simon, the Zealot

Pandemonium broke loose all over America when the U.S. hockey team defeated the Russians in the final game of the 1980 winter Olympics. People yelled, jumped up and down, doused each other with their drinks, and hugged each other for joy. I must admit that I too let out a loud whoop when the game ended. I was thrilled by our team's seemingly impossible victory.

People who exhibit such behavior in sports are called *fans*. But folks who act enthusiastically in religion are called *fanatics*. One of Jesus' apostles must have had such fervor, for he was called "Simon, the Zealot." That name is the only clue we have to his character.

Two Simons are listed among the Twelve—the well-known Simon Peter, and the obscure Simon, the Zealot. In fact, the Zealot is only mentioned in the four lists of disciples (Matt. 10:4; Mark 3:18; Luke 6:15; Acts 1:15). One tradition says he received his call to follow Jesus while fishing by the Sea of Galilee. Another popular legend identifies him as the bridegroom in the marriage in Cana.

Not only is Simon the Zealot without individual history in the New Testament, but he is listed near the end of the Twelve. In two accounts he is 11th; in the other two, 10th. Since the infamous Judas was always 12th, that makes Simon the Zealot either last or next to last. Though his rank was lowly, we should never forget that he was high among the Seventy, for Jesus did choose him to be a member of the Twelve.

His name indicates that, whether or not specially gifted, he was likely enthusiastic, fiery, ardent, and impassioned.

## He Was a Zealot

Several sects existed in the time of Jesus, including the Pharisees, the Saduccees, the Essenes, and the Zealots, last of the major parties to emerge. Simon was a member of the Zealots.

In the King James translation both Matthew and Mark speak of Simon the Canaanite, whereas later versions make a correction. The correct word is not *Kananite* (Canaanite) but *Kananaios,* which means "zealous." In fact, *Kananaios* is the Aramaic word for Zelotes, which is what Luke correctly called Simon (Luke 6:15). The wrong word *Canaanite* has geographic connotation, whereas the right word *Kananaios* carries political designation. Simon was a Jewish extremist.

The roots of the Zealots went back to 167 B.C. when an aged priest, Mattathias, raised the standard of revolt against Antioches Epiphanes in a village near Jerusalem. His five sons joined him in helping gain Jewish religious and political independence against overwhelming odds. When Mattathias died, his eldest son, Judas Maccabaeus, known as "The Hammerer," took over as leader. This brilliant Maccabean period in Jewish history came to an end with the Roman conquest.

Though well governed during an era of peace and prosperity, Palestine was always a sleeping volcano which could quickly erupt into violence. For years Herod the Great kept a quasi-peace through diplomacy by which he gained privileges from Rome for the Jews. But at his death, Palestine erupted. In Galilee an insurrectionist named Judas stormed the palace, broke into the arsenal, armed his followers, and started a short uprising. Soon after, Quirinus, the newly appointed governor over Judea, called for a census. This exploded the country into revolution, again led by Judas, who was killed in the ensuing bloodshed. From this background stemmed the group known as Zealots.

A century earlier, when Mattathias, father of the Maccabees, was dying, his parting message was, "And now, my children, be zealous for the Law, and give your lives for the covenant of your fathers" (From the Apocrypha, 1 Maccabees 2:50). Thus the Zealots derived their name as fanatical semi-revolutionaries, bitter opponents of any foreign power. Reckless and ruthless, they heroically disregarded their own interests in the struggle for their ideals.

The Zealots developed into an underground movement, capable of sabotage and violence. It is thought that Barabbas, the prisoner charged with murder and insurrection and who was released in the place of Jesus, was a Zealot. And it is not improbable that the murderers or "assassins" of Acts 21:38 were Zealots.

Historians blame the Zealots' fanaticism for bringing on the final destruction of the Jewish state. When Jerusalem was besieged in A.D. 70, the Zealots waged a virtual civil war by murdering anyone who suggested any kind of moderation of policy toward the Romans. They prolonged the siege and incurred the special wrath of their victors.

Masada, an almost impregnable fortress on the western shore of the Dead Sea, revealed their fanaticism. Nearly 1,000 inhabitants resisted the Romans to the last minute before husbands, responding to a flaming speech by their leader, killed their wives and children, then took their own lives.

These facts help us understand the background of Simon the Zealot. He was a man of passionate patriotism, a sort of freedom fighter among the Twelve, an extremist totally against the domination by Rome. His compatriots, militantly opposed to foreign taxation, hatched one conspiracy after another to promote their viewpoint, using unbridled terror in the name of religious zeal.

Picture a Zealot slipping out of his house around midnight and playing hide and seek through dark alleys to avoid enemy guards. He climbs a wall, delivers a fatal blow to a dozing Roman soldier at a remote outpost, then sneaks back home. Though Simon may not have gone that far, he was a man on record for a cause. His political adventures likely brought him much danger from time to time.

## He Was Transformed

But the most fanatic of persons may become useful in God's service. Simon was to be transformed by the Master.

*Why was Simon attracted to meek and mild Jesus?* In the first place, Jesus had great zeal. From early morning to late at night He was forever doing His Father's business, even to the sacrificial disregard of His own personal comfort. He worked so hard that one day He fell asleep in a boat in the midst of a violent storm. He bent every energy to His main goal in life. He possessed an enthusiasm which could not be doused by setbacks.

Second, Jesus spoke of a kingdom nobler than any Simon had ever dreamed of. In Simon's day, the poor were openly robbed, widows were cheated out of property, and employees were burdened by poor pay and outrageous taxes. When Jesus spoke of a golden age when Israel would no longer be oppressed, Simon listened.

Third, Simon saw Jesus' miraculous power: the sick healed, the thousands fed, the water changed into wine, and the dead raised. Simon had never witnessed such power before.

Fourth, Simon saw Jesus lash out against evil. He heard His scathing invectives pronounced on the hypocritical Pharisees. He witnessed the cleansing of the temple as Jesus overthrew tables and whipped the money-changers. Perhaps Simon misinterpreted this demonstration of zeal against dead Judaism as a revolt against Rome.

Finally, Jewish prophets had predicted a heavenly Son of man descending to earth, destroying the wicked, delivering the righteous, and reigning forever in a kingdom of holiness. Then Simon heard Jesus picture Himself coming from heaven as the Son of man (John 3:13).

Simon saw in Jesus a reformer with all the potential for revolution which he hoped would some day sweep the Romans out of Palestine. Rumors spread that the Messiah had arrived to establish His earthly throne. Even to the time of the Ascension, the disciples wouldn't give up on their concept of a political kingdom which Jesus would then restore to Israel.

*Why Jesus wanted Simon.* On the surface, the choice of

Simon seemed unwise. Wouldn't the presence of a Zealot among Jesus' official group taint His movement with political suspicion? But Jesus was never governed by the opinions of men. Through the centuries the Master has claimed, then tamed, many a fiery spirit.

Jesus' seeming disregard for prudent, worldly wisdom resulted in a cross-section of choices for His apostolic band. He didn't choose a uniform group of quiet-mannered, passive yes-men. He wanted the Twelve to be a miniature congregation, including all kinds. Simon would be qualified to reach dangerous classes.

*Reconciling opposites.* What an unlikely combination Simon and Matthew made. Matthew was sold out to Rome as a tax collector; Simon hated Rome. Matthew was a turncoat; Simon a patriot. Matthew was an instrument of burden; Simon an enemy of oppression. Had they met under other circumstances, Simon might have murdered Matthew, for Matthew was the type that ranked high on the assassin's list.

Yet Jesus bridged the deep gulf between these two men. Their personal enmity was overcome by their common love for Jesus. If these two could live at peace within that small group, then the Gospel has power to heal every dissension between men. Their harmony proved the reconciling power of the Gospel. Jesus reconciled men to Himself, then to each other.

*Sanctification of enthusiasm.* Nothing is wrong with zeal itself. The danger lies in the purpose to which it is put. Too often zeal is intellectually restricted, incapable of seeing truth in its wide ramifications. Sometimes zeal colors a person's prejudices, making him bitter. Zeal without knowledge can lead to an aggressive push of false doctrines and erroneous cults, even to inquisitions.

Misplaced zeal can make a person think he's doing God's work, while the opposite may well be true. Zealous Paul thought he was doing God a favor by harassing believers and voting for Stephen's death. His fervor took him more than 100 miles from Jerusalem to Damascus to persecute the Christians there.

But Paul later learned that zeal without knowledge is blind

and biased. Likewise Simon, whose zeal may well have been used in destructive ways, probably thought he was pleasing God. But his zeal came to be curbed, consecrated, and channeled into proper directions. If his unbounded fervor could be harnessed for the kingdom, what a spiritual freedom-fighter he would make.

The Master wanted men of strong feeling. Perhaps others of the Twelve sympathized with Zealot views, though they weren't actually members of the party. Simon's zeal served as a spark to charge the whole group. His enthusiasm was contagious, a constant challenge to the others. He never ceased to be known as "the Zealot."

*Hating into loving.* Surrendering the dagger for the Cross, Simon kept on following Jesus. He was in the Upper Room the night before the Crucifixion. He was present the first Easter night when the Lord appeared to the 10, then the next Sunday with the 11. He was present at Pentecost and on all occasions when the Twelve are collectively mentioned in Acts.

Through the transforming power of the Master, Simon's political ambitions mellowed into peaceful aspirations. The military mind gave way to missionary motivation. His view of a kingdom grew from a narrow patriotism for Judea to a passion for the whole world.

Under Jesus' teaching, Simon came to see that the great enslaving power was not Rome, but Satan and sin. Life's major struggle was not with oppressive government, but for freedom through forgiveness. After he met the Lord, Simon used his zeal to proclaim his Master's kingdom. He became gentle through association with Jesus. The man who began by hating, ended in loving.

## We Need Simon's Zeal

The apostles had a vivid model of fervor in their Master. Seeing Him in action, they recalled the Scripture, "The zeal of Thine house hath eaten me up" (Ps. 69:9; John 2:17). Fire burned in His heart, making Him a man of deep passion and warm spirit.

When he was a child, this verse once kept Theodore Roosevelt home from church because he was afraid of being eaten up by "zeal." When relating this in later years, he dryly commented that the church was now safe for small children since most of the "zeal" had disappeared from the ecclesiastical scene.

The early believers witnessed with such enthusiasm that they were called those who "turned the world upside down" (Acts 17:6). Before many decades the Gospel had secured a foothold in most of the known world. By the third century, one-tenth of the Roman empire was nominally Christian.

People exhibit zeal in many areas of life. A teenage girl submitted to rugged discipline to set three National Junior Amateur swimming records and win two National Senior swimming crowns, accumulating 60 medals along the way. She went to bed at 9 P.M. every night. Dancing, tennis, and basketball were all forbidden as they would have hardened her long, relaxed swimming muscles. During her two daily practices which totaled four hours she labored to the point of exhaustion under the tutelage of her exacting coach. She endured endless sprints, drills, and corrections. She even wore wrist splints for a while to straighten her wrists as she stroked through the water. Many of her practices were in the Potomac River against the current. Her training was so rugged that races were a relief.

Sometimes the zeal of nonbelievers surpasses that of Christians. In a parable Jesus commended an unjust steward, not for his wrongdoing but for his zealous prudence, adding, "The children of this world are in their generation wiser than the children of light" (Luke 16:8). The Lord voiced His displeasure at the lukewarmness of the Laodicean church (Rev. 3:15-16).

Enthusiasm is often considered virtuous in most lines of activity, but inappropriate if found in religion. A boy who rises at 5 A.M. to deliver handouts advertising supermarket specials is applauded as a go-getter. But if the Sunday School asked the same boy to get up early some Saturday to hand out announcements of a special church rally, people would react, "Imagine asking a boy to do that!"

When a person ties himself down to monthly payments of $100 for some luxury item, he glady pays. But when the same person puts a check for $100 on the collection plate every month, his friends may think he's crazy.

Many church members who yell like wild Indians at some game on Saturday sit like dignified wooden Indians in church on Sunday. I recall attending a Big Ten football game at Champaign, Illinois, on a cold November Saturday a few years ago. Though the temperature wasn't much above zero Fahrenheit, over 33,000 people sat in the stands. I was bundled up with a hat covering my ears, a sweater, a windbreaker, fur lined jacket, fur gloves, thermal underwear, and a blanket around my feet. I even had a thermos full of hot cocoa. The wind was blowing and the sun was hidden by clouds. The bleacher seats had been cleared of snow, but the footboards hadn't been. Then I wondered how many thousands of people would go to church and sit in heatless, near-zero sanctuaries with snow on the floor.

If a student burns the midnight oil to gain expertise in some line of knowledge, he's diligent. But if you give time to study the Bible, you're a little "different." If you have as much Christianity on Monday as you do on Sunday, you're too religious.

It was the same back in apostolic days. When Paul preached the Gospel in his defense before Agrippa, Governor Festus exclaimed loudly, "Paul, thou art beside thyself; much learning doth make thee mad!" (Acts 26:24) If Festus could speak from the dead today, he would probably be willing to change places with zealous Paul.

Many years ago Rudyard Kipling, giving the commencement address at McGill University in Montreal, warned students against over-enthusiasm for money, position, or fame. "Someday you will meet a man who cares for none of these things. Then you will know how poor you really are." *Enthuse* comes from two words meaning "in" and "God." The person who possesses divine enthusiasm is truly rich.

As a man with a sandwich board walked down the street, people snickered at the message on the front of his sign which read, "I am a fool for Christ's sake." But when they read the words on the back, they stopped their snickering, for it asked, "Whose fool are you?"

Mary lavished an expensive offering on the Lord, anointing Him with oil worth a year's wages. Paul wholeheartedly counted all things loss for Christ, and threw all his energy into spreading the Good News of Christ. Likewise the apostles discovered a love so overwhelming they could not refrain from full consecration.

Missionaries have exhausted themselves for God, like Henry Martyn of Cambridge University, who reached the shores of India and made this entry in his journal, "I desire to burn out for God." Spurgeon said that in his opinion earnestness was the most essential quality in winning souls. When a church leader was asked how his church could be helped spiritually, he answered, "Send us an enthusiast, someone with zeal!"

Paul urged, "And whatsoever ye do, do it heartily, as to the Lord" (Col. 3:23). Peter encouraged us to be followers of that which is good, which is translated by the *Revised Standard Version*, "zealous for what is right," and by J. B. Phillips, "enthusiastic for good" (1 Peter 3:13).

Simon the Zealot was the type who could get all excited about Jesus. After all, when we become graphically aware that our sins are forgiven and forgotten, that heaven is our sure home some day, that in every trial we have a Saviour who can see us through, shouldn't we be inwardly leaping for joy? Wouldn't we be more like Simon if we could get less concerned about things that matter little, and more excited about things that really count for eternity?

## Simon's Martyrdom

Many legends surround Simon's missionary journeys. He supposedly preached the Gospel in Asia Minor, northern Africa, the Black Sea area, and Babylon. Some accounts say he was murdered by a mob in Persia. Stories also persist that his travels took him to Britain. His symbol is a fish lying on a Bible, which indicates that a fisherman became a fisher of men through preaching the Word.

Simon is a rebuke to our coldness and spiritual paralysis. We need to pray,

Come Holy Spirit, heavenly
  Dove
With all Thy quickening power,
Kindle a flame of sacred love
In these cold hearts of ours.

# 12

## Judas, the Traitor

Though the artist El Greco was commissioned by church authorities to do a painting of each of the apostles individually, he never did a separate portrait of Judas, for he considered him an unworthy subject. In fact, in his painting, *Christ at Gethsemane*, which captures the dramatic moment just before the betrayal, he makes Judas barely visible in the lower right corner.

Judas is the epitome of treachery. *Webster's New Collegiate Dictionary* says of his name: "Traitor, especially one who betrays under the guise of friendship." Mountains of vile epithets have been hurled against him in the literature of the centuries. Folklore always makes him the villain.

Our daily vocabulary reflects the infamy of this tragic apostle. *Judas-colored* refers to red hair, which tradition ascribes to him. *Judas tree*, a purple-blossomed tree, is believed to be the kind on which he hanged himself. The stockyard animal used to lead its fellow animals to the slaughter is termed the *Judas goat*. A seemingly friendly act that turns out to be a stab in the back is called the *Judas kiss*. *Judas Priest* is a profane substitute for Jesus Christ, an exclamation of disgust or irritation. A *Judas hole* is a peephole in a prison door that permits a person to see into the cell without being seen by the prisoner inside.

The reason for the anathematizing of his name is found in the

New Testament. In every list of the apostles, Judas was undisputed holder of the last position (Matt. 10:4; Mark 3:19; Luke 6:16). Over and over he was identified as the one who would or did betray Jesus (Matt. 10:4; 26:25; 27:3; Mark 3:19; Luke 6:16; John 6:71; 12:4; 18:2, 5). What a nickname to stick for over 1900 years—"The Traitor."

The honor of his apostleship throws his disgrace into starker contrast. In recounting the betrayal, all three Synoptic gospels specify that he was "one of the Twelve" (Matt. 26:47; Mark 14:10, 43, Luke 22:3, 47). Imagine—the betrayer came from among the Lord's closest friends.

The story of Judas raises many puzzing questions. Why did Jesus choose a person like Judas? Was Jesus aware of the danger from the beginning? If not, when did He become aware? Was there any way Jesus could have handled Judas to forestall what Judas did? Was Judas predestined to be the betrayer, and thus forced to play that part?

## Judas' High Honor

Judas started out well. His beginning had all the elements of nobility. Judas was once a proud name, a form of Judah, which means "praised." Judas Maccabaeus, who led his people in revolt against their Macedonian oppressors, was a great national hero like George Washington. Jesus had a brother named Judas (Matt. 13:55), who probably wrote the Epistle of Jude. Another of the Twelve bore the same name but was differentiated from the traitor (John 14:22).

Judas Iscariot is thought to be a corruption of Judas Ish Kerioth, a man of Kerioth, a small town a few miles south of Hebron. This would make him the only apostle not a Galilean. As a Judean, perhaps he did not share a closeness with the others. This could have made him more vulnerable to disloyalty, and could have explained his affinity with the scribes and Pharisees. His father's name was Simon (John 13:2).

*Potential.* Judas was not a traitor when Jesus chose him. To depict him as an unkempt hoodlum, lurking in the bushes with a threatening stare and an assassin's intent, is to forget he must have been an average man, much like the people who sit beside us in church.

The fact that Jesus selected him indicates Judas possessed the same potential as the other disciples. Remember, Jesus had spent all the previous night in prayer before picking the Twelve (Luke 6:12-16). He chose carefully from among a wider group of disciples. To all appearances Judas was a most eligible candidate, a man of promise with high ideals.

Jesus chose Judas to be an apostle, not a traitor. Judas made his own choice to be a traitor.

*Privileges.* Like the other apostles, Judas forsook all to follow Jesus. For three years he was a close associate of the Lord. He walked and talked with the Son of God. He sat under the stars with Him, broke bread with Him, and listened to Him.

Judas heard the Sermon on the Mount, and also the probing parables. He saw the blind receive sight, the deaf hear, and the dead rise. He was in the presence of Him who stilled the storm, cast out demons, chased the racketeers out of the temple, and took little children in His arms to bless them.

Judas even went on a preaching mission for the Lord and was used to cast out demons (Luke 10:17-20). These transcendental privileges were given Judas just as to the rest of the Twelve.

*Position as Treasurer.* The choice of Judas as treasurer of the Twelve showed that his companions had a lot of confidence in him (John 12:6). Though Matthew had ample experience with money as a tax collector, Judas must have displayed some financial expertise. Also, he won their respect as trustworthy and responsible. By common consent he handled the bag into which went all gifts and from which came all expenditures. He never gave the slightest hint that he would eventually pilfer funds. He was careful, capable, businesslike, and honest—at least at the beginning.

## Judas' Drastic Downfall

An artist was commissioned to paint in a Sicilian cathedral a mural depicting the life of Jesus. He discovered a 12-year-old boy whose radiant innocence made a perfect model for the

Christ-child. Years later, the artist had developed the mural to the events of Holy Week with major figures completed, except for Judas. One afternoon a man whose face showed the results of excessive drinking staggered into a tavern where the artist was sitting. Immediately the artist chose the wino as a perfect model for the remaining figure. Leading the man to the cathedral, he pointed to the bare space on the wall and asked him to pose for Judas. The derelict broke out in sobs, "Don't you remember me?" Pointing to the Christ-child, he explained, "I was your model for Him many years ago!"

Think what Judas could have become. Like the faithful 11 he could have gone out to sacrificial service, notable martyrdom, and merited rewards in heaven. Cities, churches, and children have been named after the other apostles. Their names are written in the Book of Life and will be inscribed on the 12 foundations of the New Jerusalem (Rev. 21:14). Judas could have been remembered as a great missionary-apostle, but instead he is known as the traitor.

The story of Judas is often repeated. A person can be numbered with the people of God, serve on church boards, be active on committees, take communion, but go out to covetous practices and raw business deals, and at last to a lost eternity—right from church. Even after associating with Christ and His followers we can harbor a devil in our hearts. Though no one is asked today to deliver Christ bodily into enemy hands, nevertheless people do betray Him in more subtle ways.

## Explaining Judas' Downfall

Many attempts have been made to whitewash Judas' despicable deed. Some comment that his return to the Sanhedrin proves him the only one to plead Jesus' innocence before that austere body. But Judas' return to the Sanhedrin highlights his guilt more than Jesus' innocence.

Suggested explanations of Judas' tragedy can be classified in one of three categories: those that place the blame lightly on Judas, those that excuse him completely, and those that put responsibility solely on Judas.

Those who hold Judas only mildly guilty picture him as a misguided patriot who meant well by his act of betrayal. They believe that Judas hoped that putting his Master in a difficult spot would force Him to become a militant Messiah. Cornered into declaring His kingship, Jesus would then have used His superhuman powers to save Himself and take over the throne of Israel. This view holds that Judas never dreamed Jesus would be crucified, but would rather save the day by giving a bona fide demonstration of His power. In the same vein, *Jesus Christ Superstar* and Hugh J. Schonfield's *The Passover Plot* both make Judas look like a misunderstood hero. But Jesus called him "a devil" and "the son of perdition" (John 6:70; 17:12).

Those who exonerate Judas completely, virtually blame God. In their view Judas was a scapegoat, playing the role assigned him by God's providence. He was chosen to be the traitor, just as an actor might be given the villain's part. Bluntly, he was predestined to do this dastardly deed, and should be excused, for he couldn't help it. But such reasoning fails to explain why Judas condemned himself, moaning, "I have betrayed the innocent blood" (Matt. 27:3-4). He knew it was his own fault. In the post-resurrection Upper Room, Peter prayed before the vote for a successor to Judas concerning the "apostleship, from which Judas by transgression fell, that he might go to his own place" (Acts 1:25). To the place of his own choice. He was responsible for his transgression.

The Bible teaches both God's predestination and man's free will. The story of Judas is an example of how God's sovereignty and man's responsibility blend in the same incident. Jesus said of him, "The Son of man indeed goeth, as it is written of Him: but woe to that man by whom the Son of man is betrayed! Good were it for that man if he had never been born" (Mark 14:21). Jesus meant that His betrayal was part of the divine plan for Him in His redemption of mankind. He also taught that the part Judas played was so heinous that it would have been better had Judas never been born. Yet though the betrayal was in the plan of God, Judas was responsible for his choice in becoming the betrayer. Someone had to sell Jesus out to the religious leaders, but it was Judas who chose to become that someone. He decided his destiny.

## Steps in Judas' Downfall

If Judas bears responsibility for his horrible crime, how did he slip so badly? What factors contributed to his downfall?

In 1776 Benedict Arnold, commander of West Point, secretly offered to surrender West Point to the British for 20,000 pounds. What caused this man to become a traitor? Winston Churchill in his *History of the English Speaking Peoples* cites these reasons: dissatisfaction with the conduct of American troops, marriage to a loyalist lady, indebtedness, and a recent reprimand at a court-martial for misappropriation of government property. Interestingly, two of these reasons are strikingly similar to those accounting for Judas' downfall.

*Judas' growing disenchantment with Jesus.* Villains don't blossom overnight. Judas' nefarious deed was not a sudden plunge, but the last of several steps in his gradual descent to the waters of depravity. When he left all to follow Jesus, he never dreamed he would be a betrayer. But somewhere along the line, he slowly began to slip. Jesus could sense what was happening and issued several warnings.

Judas was looking for an earthly kingdom. He thought Jesus would deliver the Jewish nation from the Romans and establish His Messianic rule on earth. Judas expected to share in the glory and power of this new government.

But then Judas heard things which didn't quite fit with his concept of Jesus' mission: that advice of turning the other cheek, of not worrying about tomorrow, of not laying up treasures on earth, and of loving your enemies. After the feeding of the 5,000 Jesus said some things that made many fringe followers leave. But Peter told Jesus, "Lord, to whom shall we go? Thou hast the words of eternal life" (John 6:68).

At that point Jesus gave a direct warning to Judas, "Have not I chosen you twelve, and one of you is a devil?" In his record John added, from the vantage of history, "He spake of Judas Iscariot the son of Simon: for he it was that should betray Him, one of the Twelve" (vv. 70-71).

How did Jesus know? Perhaps through His omniscience, plus His observance in Judas of uneasiness at His teachings, slackening interest in prayer, resentments, and covetousness.

When Jesus kept predicting His coming death, it became evident to Judas that Jesus' kingdom was not political but spiritual. Instead of sitting on a glorious throne, Jesus would die an ignominious death. As enemies began to plot against Jesus, Judas could see all his aspirations blowing up in his face.

*Judas' covetousness.* Another factor that led to his downfall was avarice. When Mary anointed Jesus with expensive perfume, Judas criticized the act as waste: "Why was not this ointment sold for three hundred pence, and given to the poor?" John added, again from the vantage point of history, "This he said, not that he cared for the poor; but because he was a thief, and had the bag, and bare what was put therein" (John 12:4-6). Immediately Jesus defended Mary, "Quit criticizing her. She has done this in anticipation of my burial" (see v. 7). The reader of human hearts knew Judas' motive was evil, but Mary's noble.

The 10th commandment, "Thou shalt not covet," seems inoffensive. But it's really crucial, for its leads to a host of sins. Coveting a neighbor's reputation may lead to slander and lies. Coveting a neighbor's possessions may lead to theft. Coveting a neighbor's mate may lead to adultery. Coveting something badly enough may lead to murder. For Judas, it led to the crucifixion of Jesus. "The love of money is the root of all evil" (1 Tim. 6:10).

How often Judas had heard Jesus warn against the love of money. "You cannot serve God and mammon" (Matt. 6:24; Luke 16:13). Jesus began one of His parables, "Beware of covetousness" (Luke 12:15). Before we condemn Judas too strongly, remember that the person who misuses his time, talents, gifts, opportunities, or money robs God too.

Judas' growing disillusionment with Jesus' intentions and his greed set the stage for the betrayal. Harboring a quiet, morose grudge against his Master, Judas saw a way to salvage something out of Jesus' impending disaster. If he could betray Jesus to the establishment, Judas would save his own skin and get some money out of it as well. Succumbing to the temptation, Judas "went . . . and communed with the chief priests and captains, how he might betray Him unto them. And they were glad, and covenanted to give him money. And he promised, and sought opportunity to betray Him unto them in the absence of the multitude" (Luke 22:4-6).

So heinous was this action that Luke prefaced it, "Then entered Satan into Judas" (22:3). To express his horror, John twice mentioned the devil in the betrayal account (John 13:2, 27). Judas opened the door to Satan.

What trifles people sell Jesus for today—a job, a bit of pleasure, a friendship, a few dollars. A farmer drove his truck onto the grain elevator scales, then sneakily walked on the scales himself. The operator noted the total weight on the scales credit form. Handing it to the farmer, he remarked, "You just sold yourself for $10."

## More Warnings for Judas

In the Upper Room Passover observance, Jesus warned Judas at least three times. Judas had to be there to find out the whereabouts of his Master later that night. Jesus would not allow Judas to carry out his terrible plan without a final appeal. He could have exposed the traitor at the very start, dismissing him from the group. But instead Jesus treated him with loving courtesy all through the meal, giving him every chance to repent.

Jesus' first warning came at the washing of His disciples' feet. As Jesus looked up from Judas' feet into his hard face, He looked for some small sign of repentance. When none showed, Jesus warned, " 'He that is washed needeth not save to wash his feet, but is clean every whit; and ye are clean, but not all.' For He knew who should betray Him; therefore He said, 'Ye are not all clean' " (John 13:10-11). Judas must have sat tense and uncomfortable, but he only hardened his heart more.

Jesus' second warning came during the Passover meal. All four Gospels record the bombshell the Master dropped by announcing that one of them would betray Him (Matt. 26:21; Mark 14:18; Luke 22:21; John 13:21). Shocked and stunned into silence, they then broke into questions, "Lord, is it I?" No one pointed to Judas, "Is it he?" To the others Judas was still above suspicion. Jesus hoped that Judas would sense the enormity of his atrocity by the other disciples' horrified reactions. Instead Judas hypocritically asked, "Is it I?" Jesus replied, in effect, "It is as you have spoken" (Matt. 26:25). Due to Judas' proximity to Jesus, apparently the others didn't hear.

Still a third warning came as a result of Peter's gesture to John to ask who the traitor was. Apparently John sat at one side of Jesus and Judas at the other. Jesus answered John, "He it is, to whom I shall give a sop, when I have dipped it." Then Jesus dipped the sop and gave it to Judas Iscariot (John 13:23-26). Since John's question may have been whispered in Jesus' ear, the others may not have known the significance of the sop-giving, thinking it the custom to give the first sop to the guest of honor. Receiving the "guest of honor" sop should have melted Judas' conscience. But this one last appeal had no outward effect.

Judas probably knew that John now knew. In a mixture of fear and resentment at the exposure, Judas responded to the impulse of the devil and left immediately. Seeing he was determined to carry out the bargain, Jesus said, "That thou doest, do quickly" (John 13:27). The other disciples thought Judas was leaving to perform some "treasurer" assignment. The door closed. Judas went out. "And it was night" (v. 30). Not only night outside, but a desperate, deeper night within Judas' heart.

## The Kiss

Judas knew the secret place of prayer where the group would go later. How often he had been there with the Master (John 18:2). So he went to tell the religious leaders and to collect his 30 pieces of silver.

Later in Gethsemane, after a period of agonizing prayer, Jesus woke His sleeping disciples, " 'Rise, let us be going: behold, he is at hand that doth betray Me.' And while He yet spake, lo, Judas, one of the Twelve, came, and with him a great multitude with swords and staves from the chief priests and elders of the people. Now he that betrayed Him gave them a sign, saying, 'Whomsoever I shall kiss, that same is He: hold Him fast.' And forthwith he came to Jesus, and said, 'Hail Master;' and kissed Him" (Matt. 26:46-49).

It was customary for a disciple on meeting a rabbi to put his hands on the master's shoulder and to kiss him. This was the agreed sign. The original language indicated that Judas' kiss was a hearty one. Betraying by a kiss is like using a friendly cup of coffee to poison a dear friend.

At this point those about to arrest Jesus fell backward to the ground (John 18:3-6). Was this demonstration of power the final appeal?

## Judas' Tragic End

Judas could have been forgiven, like Peter. He could have gone to Jesus and asked pardon. When a Dutch priest who had survived the Nazi occupation spoke of the Nazis in terms of forgiveness, a friend rebuked him, "You're too kind. You forget what they did. You would have a good word even for a condemned soul like Judas." Whereupon the priest, placing his hand on his friend's arm, answered earnestly, "If Judas, in that terrible moment when he hanged himself, and just before he lost consciousness entirely, sighed his regret and his repentance, I assure you that the sigh was heard in heaven and that the first drop of Jesus' blood was shed for Judas Iscariot."

Peter repented, but Judas did not. Illustrating the difference, Dr. Donald G. Barnhouse told of two ministers, both of whom had wandered from the Lord. One, Mel Dibble, had been an assistant pastor in a large Michigan church, then later a soloist in Barnhouse's Philadelphia church. Barnhouse related how during the National Association of Evangelicals' annual convention in Cincinnati, he took Dibble out to dinner. Dibble was then a popular emcee on a network TV program originating from Cincinnati. He admitted to Barnhouse that he was deeply backslidden.

Barnhouse told Dibble a story he had heard from Billy Graham that very afternoon. Graham had been preaching in Chattanooga. In that city lived a Baptist evangelist who had fallen into deep sin. Someone got him to attend the Graham meeting.

The ex-evangelist sat in the front row. Under his breath he kept repeating, "I used to have crowds like this. People used to listen to me like this."

When the meeting finished, the ex-preacher walked to a secondhand store, bought a revolver, and put it to his temple. He pulled the trigger, but his aim was bad. Instead of killing himself, he shot out both his eyes.

That night after Barnhouse and Dibble had dinner, Dibble attended the NAE service where Graham was speaking. Later in a hotel room, Dibble came back to the Lord. He literally walked away from his TV program and has been active in evangelism ever since.

Dibble repented, but as far as is known, the blind ex-preacher never did. Peter repented, but Judas did not. Judas had remorse, but did not sorrow unto repentance. After Jesus' arrest, Judas doubtless lurked in the shadows much of the night. When in the morning he learned that Jesus was condemned, he was sorry. The 30 pieces of silver began to burn in his grasp.

Hurrying back to the council, he burst into the hall, moaning, "I have sinned in that I have betrayed innocent blood." They mocked, "What is that to us? See thou to that." Then Judas threw down the pieces of silver in the temple and went to hang himself. The chief priests, unable to place blood money in the treasury, purchased a potter's field in which to bury strangers (Matt. 27:3-10).

Not a hardened criminal, undoubtedly influenced by the teachings and companionship of Jesus, Judas could not help but have felt guilty. But it wasn't full repentance. Some people are sorry for their wrongs because they get caught, because they get satiated with their pleasures, or because they are disappointed over results that don't measure up to their anticipation. But that's not repentance.

Judas remembered a nearby cliff on which stood a tree. Throwing a rope over a branch, he fastened it tightly, knotted the other end around his neck, then jumped. Another account of Judas' death, given by Peter in the Upper Room reads, "falling headlong, he burst asunder in the midst, and all his bowels gushed out" (Acts 1:18). Some early writers thought the tragedy resulted from a disease which caused his stomach to swell grossly, or from a crushing caused by a wagon running over him. Some critics claim a contradiction in the two accounts of his death. The Vulgate renders Acts 1:18, "When he had hanged himself, he burst assunder," suggesting a possible harmonization. First, he hanged himself. Then somehow his body toppled over the cliff causing a stomach wound.

Peter ended his Upper Room speech by saying Judas went to his own place (Acts 1:25). He might have taken the Gospel to Greece, or Egypt, or India, or Asia Minor as did other apostles. But instead he forfeited his ministry to go to a lost eternity. Jesus had indirectly declared his lack of salvation when He said, "None of them is lost, but the son of perdition" (John 17:12). Tragically, his defection changed the name of the Twelve. Luke records that after the Resurrection the *Eleven* were gathered together (24:33).

Judas' symbol is a hangman's noose, or a money purse with a piece of silver falling from it. Sometimes the emblem is completely blank, indicating no influence for good.

One lesson from Judas' tragedy is that a downfall may be hidden from others for a long time, because it starts and progresses inside our hearts till the day it breaks out into open evil. Sin may lurk privately long before it goes public.

In 1975 people in Mountainside, New Jersey were amazed when a likeable 15-year-old boy from a church-going family murdered both his parents with an axe, then jumped to his death from a 150-foot water tower. After the funeral, police discovered a secret room over the porch of the house which could only be entered by crawling through a small opening in the boy's bedroom. Inside the hideout he had smuggled, not only a lamp and mattress, but a collection of Nazi materials—a swastika-decorated two-foot panel, several swastika armbands, and a six-page handwritten paper of quotations of Hitler, which the boy had copied himself. This paraphernalia had nourished the boy's thought-life until it finally exhibited itself in his chilling behavior.

What of you and me? We have the words of Christ. We know our duty. Do we let Him change us? Or do we go right on calling Him, "Lord, Lord," but fail to do the things He asks? Our response will decide whether we will be remembered with Judas Iscariot or not.

One fall a visitor at West Point Military Academy noticed the number *12* placed all around the campus on large banners. Asking for an explanation, he was told, "A football team has 11 players. There are 11 men playing the game for Army. The number *12* is symbolic of the *12th man,* standing for the rest of the student body, whose support is as important for victory as the team itself." Because of a recent lack of school spirit, West Point had initiated an all-out campaign to encourage the enthusiasm of all the students—the *12th* man.

When Judas ended his life, eleven men were left. Though Matthias was voted to replace him, in a sense we as believers could consider ourselves the *12th* apostle, and thus assume our responsibility for getting the Gospel out to our Jerusalems, Samarias, and to the ends of the earth.

"As the Father hath sent Me," says our Master, "even so send I you" (John 20:21).

**Additional Victor books written by Leslie Flynn include:**

**The Gift of Joy**
How do you find joy? How are joy and happiness related? How are they different? In this book, Dr. Flynn dispels the myths that joy equals happiness and that grumpiness equals holiness.

**God's Will: You Can Know It**
How do you go about finding God's will? How can you be a decisive person—yet at the same time know you are following God's leading? From biblical principles—and the experiences of people of the past and present—you can learn how to let God direct you.

**Joseph: God's Man in Egypt**
Joseph was a perfect candidate for anger, despair, revenge, and self-pity. Yet Joseph's life offers hope—you too can live with courage and faith when everything around you goes wrong.

**19 Gifts of the Spirit**
Examine the gifts and special abilities given to Christians by the Holy Spirit. Which ones do you have? Are you using them? Dr. Flynn guides you in an in-depth study of what the Bible says about spiritual gifts.

**Dare to Care Like Jesus**
You can develop greater compassion as you follow the example Jesus set in His tears, anger, patience, gratitude, approachability, loneliness, humor, submissiveness, and graciousness.